The Kindergarten Dropout of Kapoho

THE HALI'A ALOHA SERIES

The Kindergarten Dropout of Kapoho

FRANCES H. KAKUGAWA

LEGACY ISLE
PUBLISHING

THE HALI'A ALOHA SERIES
Darien Hsu Gee, Series Editor

Hali'a Aloha ("cherished memories") by Legacy Isle Publishing is a guided memoir program developed in collaboration with series editor Darien Hsu Gee. The series celebrates moments big and small, harnessing the power of short forms to preserve the lived experiences of the storytellers. To become a Hali'a Aloha author, please visit www.legacyislepublishing.net.

Legacy Isle Publishing is an imprint of Watermark Publishing, based in Honolulu, Hawai'i, and dedicated to "Telling Hawai'i's Stories" through memoirs, corporate biographies, family histories and other books.

© 2020 Frances H. Kakugawa

All rights reserved. No part of this book may be reproduced in any form or by any electronic or mechanical means, including information retrieval systems, without prior written permission from the publisher, except for brief passages quoted in reviews.

Most of the names in this book have been changed to protect the privacy of the individuals involved.

ISBN 978-1-948011-43-3 (print)
ISBN 978-1-948011-44-0 (ebook)

Design and production
Dawn Sakamoto Paiva

Legacy Isle Publishing
1000 Bishop St., Ste. 806
Honolulu, HI 96813
Telephone 1-808-587-7766
Toll-free 1-866-900-BOOK
www.legacyislepublishing.net

Printed in the United States

This book is dedicated to
the memory of my parents
—Sadame and Matsue Kakugawa—
and my grandparents
—Sampachi Kakugawa and Matsuno Ikeda,
Nobuichi and Tsune Takahashi—
and to all my ancestors buried in
Hawaiʻi and in Hiroshima

Also by Frances H. Kakugawa

POETRY

Sand Grains

White Ginger Blossoms

Golden Spike

The Path of Butterflies

Dangerous Woman: Poetry for the Ageless

CAREGIVING

Mosaic Moon: Caregiving through Poetry

Breaking the Silence: A Caregiver's Voice

*I Am Somebody:
Bringing Dignity and Compassion
to Alzheimer's Caregiving*

MEMOIRS

Teacher, You Look Like a Horse!

Kapoho: Memoir of a Modern Pompeii

Echoes of Kapoho: A Memoir

CHILDREN'S BOOKS

Wordsworth the Poet

Wordsworth Dances the Waltz

Wordsworth! Stop the Bulldozer!

Wordsworth, It's In Your Pocket!

CONTENTS

Introduction 1
Eh! You Tink You Haole? 3
The Kindergarten Dropout of Kapoho 10
The Emperor's Kidnapped Daughter 15
It Was Once Upon a Time 23
Taxi Money 31
A Kapoho Christmas 37
Mrs. Honda's Beautiful Daughter 39
There Was a Man Named Davi 47
The Unfinished Dance 52
You Look Like, You Look Like… 60
The Porch 70
The Eastern Way 81
Wordsworth and Me 86
Girl of Kapoho 93
Dear Kapoho 94
The New Kapoho, 2018 104
Glossary 109
Acknowledgments 110
Publication Notes 111

INTRODUCTION

One of the stories in my 2011 memoir, *Kapoho: Memoir of a Modern Pompeii*, ends with a celebratory "I'm out!"

I had finally severed my umbilical cord with help from Goddess Pele. With her blessing, I would now remain a step ahead of the next lava flow. I would look at the sky with that strange sense of fire, sniffing the breeze like the dogs of Kapoho for a sense of the next eruption. Sometimes it was just the sweeping beacon from Kapoho's lighthouse disguising Pele's flare, or a ghost from the cemetery. My escape from the sounds of the last eruption and the tongues of lava lapping at my heels would lead me to my own human landscape in a new world. Fire hereafter would always be the fire of passion, determined and orchestrated by the emperor's daughter. Goodbye, Kapoho.

Is that laughter coming from the fire pit of Kīlauea? Are you joining Pele's laughter, having known right along that once you're a Kapoho girl, you can't be anything else? And is that really a bad thing? The war that confused me at age five would reappear throughout my life with a different face. Life after Kapoho was not always that glamorous cocktail party of my childhood fantasies. There would be many challenges and tribulations, from sexual harassment to racism. But there would also be empowerment and dreams that could be fulfilled with tools lying at arm's reach—a bag of Kapoho survival skills and my pen.

I hope you enjoy this journey out of and back to our modern-day Pompeii. For no matter how far I travel, these stories echo the experiences and spirit of old Kapoho.

EH! YOU TINK YOU HAOLE?

"Eh! You tink you haole?" This was the ultimate put-down. "You think you're white?" Whites were the plantation managers in our village, movie stars, mainlanders and fancy-dressed city slickers. They spoke proper English, were well mannered, sat at tables covered with white linen tablecloths, used napkins instead of sleeves and ate with forks, spoons and knives, and by candlelight. We were locals.

Pidgin has limitless ways to say exactly what we want to:

"What? You tink you fut perfume? You think you shit ice cream?" Haoles did both, of course. By candlelight, they were an evolutionary step beyond us.

We have a saying in Hawai'i: "Put a bunch of crabs in a bucket, and when one tries to climb out, the others will pull it down."

I planned to get out of Kapoho to reach that star I'd hung my dream on since first grade. It was a very deep bucket, but I was going to get out. But how was I going to become a great writer with a mouthful of pidgin? I had to start speaking "like a haole." That would mean being different. That would mean, "Eh, you tink you haole?"

My earliest recollection of the printed word was when I was five years old. I watched my oldest brother go through the *Hilo Tribune-Herald*, turning the pages without reading each article.

"How come he not reading every word? If I know how to read, I goin' read every word." I later took the newspaper and read all the "the" words. "The" was the only printed word I knew.

I learned to read in first grade—that is, more than "the." I was delighted. It was pure magic to read about Dick, Jane and Sally with Spot and Sally's teddy bear Tim. I could read! I ached for their little red wagon, a wish I held throughout my childhood years. In the end, I had to settle for red Saturns and Hondas. Life-changing magic happened one day in first grade. I heard my first poem. The teacher read a poem about flowers speaking to each other. I saw visions of flowers with faces painted with long black eyelashes and red smiling lips. I was totally captivated. I fell in love with words and their magic and vowed that I would someday become a writer.

I read a lot. I immersed myself in the world of language. I wanted something more than Kapoho, and language was my ticket. I had to learn to speak correctly if I were to follow my dream. I would be different. It was my secret, and I never explained it to anyone.

The boys in my classroom read my silence and understood my dream. Instead of putting me down for "talking like a haole," they surprised me. Each time I spoke in Standard English, they told me, "Yeah, you goin' college."

My face was often in a book, and I seldom joined my classmates in games. The boys said, "She goin' college." The girls shook their heads and left me alone.

On the last day of sixth grade, a group of boys watched me walk out of the school grounds, and I heard one voice yell, "Hey, college girl, you goin' college, man." My heart inflated like a balloon that never popped until I took Speech 100 in college. One of the boys was sixteen years old. He wasn't going to college; he wasn't even going to junior high. He had waited to be sixteen so that by law, he could drop out of school.

Talking haole is easier said than done. My three teachers from the first through sixth grades were high school graduates from the village, without college degrees. They read to us daily and tried anything and everything to help us grow beyond the limited world of Kapoho.

Our homes had no telephones, so in school, the teachers used role-playing to teach us telephone etiquette.

"Hello."

"Hello. May I speak to John, please?"

"One moment, please."

Instead of:

"Eh, I like talk to John."

"Wait, eh, I go call 'em."

Teachers brought in olives and cheese to give us a taste for haole cuisine. I met a teacher forty years later, and she told her own story of being shocked that many of her students had never tasted olives. Olives would later become "holiday food" on Christmas and New Year's Day.

Two words tripped me up constantly and became my nemeses: "hospital" and "volcano." I added extra syllables to them. "Her father was ill so he went to the 'ha-see-pee-tall'" and "The 'vo-lo-cay-no' is erupting." Each time I mispronounced these words, my name went up in lights on the blackboard. At the end of the day, there was a tally after my name for all mispronounced words.

I stayed after school and pronounced each word twenty times for each tally. "Volcano, volcano, volcano, hospital, hospital, hospital..." The following day, "ha-see-pee-tall" and "vo-lo-cay-no" came rolling off my tongue, uncontrollable lava, heated with frustration.

I spent many afternoons repeating these words over and over again, but the "th" sound was my Everest.

"Stick your tongue out between your teeth when you say the 'th' sound in 'the, there, this, father, mother,'" the teacher instructed. I placed my tongue between my teeth, pulled it back in and said, "Da, dere, dis, fadda, madda." I stuck my tongue out a lot learning to speak right. I didn't mind. I was learning to speak haole, where my dreams lived.

I began my freshman year at the two-year University of Hawai'i campus in Hilo. Making a living now had to be part of the mix of becoming a writer. A detour through the College of Education seemed the best way to do both.

But my Standard English interlaced with pidgin created an insurmountable barrier to my career plans. The University of Hawai'i required that we pass the Speech Board to qualify for other speech courses as a prerequisite to enrolling in the College of Education. Bonehead Speech 100 was my first stop.

After Speech 100, I faced the Speech Board at the end of the semester and failed. My pidgin dialect gave me away. I stood there dumbfounded. After all my years of practice, I still couldn't speak like a haole. I should have taken up accounting.

A board member from the Mānoa campus on O'ahu suggested that I attend a speech clinic for a semester and try again. He gave me his home telephone number and said, "Call me when you transfer to the main campus."

I transferred to the main campus, attended the speech clinic and once again stood before the Speech Board. One of the board members (not my friend, of course) burst into laughter after my short speech. "My God," he said, "How did she end up with a Southern accent?"

Oh, shit, I thought frantically. *Now I have two dialects!*

The tutor at the speech clinic was from the South. The board members conferred and let it go; I was headed for Speech 105. Whew! I left before they could change their minds. I walked toward the door, turned around and said, "Bye, y'all," and smiled back at them. Some students weren't as fortunate and were forced to switch career plans.

Three and a half years after receiving my teaching degree, I taught for a year at a Michigan elementary school. Faculty members were intrigued by my New England dialect. I was a carrier of Hawaiʻi's history of missionaries who had arrived from New England after Captain Cook. At the end of the school year, the principal confessed that a teacher had been assigned to observe me because my first graders were the best behaved, and the other faculty members were interested in my technique. "It was your use of language," the principal said.

"Our kids are always rowdy after recess. We watched you stand at the door after recess. You just point your thumb toward your door and quietly say, 'In' or 'Recess is over.' Your kids all settle down and walk in quietly. It was the same at assemblies and on field trips. Your students are the best behaved."

The entire faculty, I learned, began to speak in shorter sentences instead of rambling on and on about how recess was over and the children needed to get into the classroom. She chuckled, "We learned not to over-talk because kids stopped listening to us, but we noticed, as the year went along, that your sentences were getting longer as ours got shorter." Was I finally speaking like a haole?

After I returned to Hawaiʻi, a debate on pidgin versus Standard English plagued me during my years of teaching.

"No! No! No!" argued the linguists. "A dialect ought not to be tampered with and should be part of our language in and out of school."

"It might save the culture," I replied, "but it didn't save me." I wouldn't allow pidgin in my classroom. My students were free to speak any language or dialect outside of the classroom. But I was determined not to have any speech board crush the aspirations of my students. Not on my watch. The linguists need not have worried. My native use of pidgin still screws me up. And my sentences are as short as ever.

Five years ago, I returned to the Islands for a funeral. Three old Kapoho friends came up to me after the service.

"Eh, you da Kakugawa girl, eh?"

"Eh, we read about you all da time. We have all your books, you know."

"We so proud of you. Man, you some famous. We see you on TV all da time."

"No, not famous," I said. "And hey, we all came from the same outhouse." We laughed and talked story about Kapoho and the good old days before it was destroyed by lava.

One of these old friends had a special place in my heart. He had lifted me up to the rim of the bucket. "Go speak like one haole," he had said, "because you goin' college."

THE KINDERGARTEN DROPOUT OF KAPOHO

I was a kindergarten dropout. There was no other choice—it was either drop out of kindergarten or go to jail for the rest of my life.

On the first day of school, students were running around the classroom. My neighbor Sammy was on top of a table trying to escape the teacher. I was envious as he leaped from table to table, Gene Kelly fashion, laughing and having the time of his life. Other kids were running around the lower decks, knocking down chairs and playing tag. In the free-for-all room, I stood like a statue, wishing I could be running around. This would not be the first time I would feel inadequate, that I was not being raised right by my parents.

"How come I don't know how to run around like Sammy?" But before I could find an answer, fear overtook me and froze me in my chair. The person I had learned to fear most stood in the doorway.

I watched the teacher approach the silhouette in the doorway. They spoke in muted tones to each other. They turned back toward the class, and I felt their eyes on me. He had come for me.

"Why dey lookin' at me? He goin' take me to jail." The fear of the policeman accompanied me for the rest of the day. I needed to get out of there. I wanted to go home. He was taking me to jail. That was what policemen did. I wanted my mother.

Kindergarten was not compulsory in the 1940s. Pāhoa School was seven miles from where we lived. They added kindergarten classes for the first time that year, and I became the first victim. My mother offered me a bribe I couldn't refuse.

"Oh, you're so lucky," my mother said. "You and Sammy will be the first two from Kapoho to go to kindergarten. How lucky. You'll get to ride the bus with all the big people."

"No, I not going. I staying home with you."

"You can wear a new dress every day."

It would mean riding the Higashi bus, which made one daily round trip from Kapoho to Hilo. We would be dropped off at Pāhoa School and picked up in the afternoon, which meant that I would be stuck in school for the whole day with no way to escape. It also meant that I would be riding with adults and older students whom I didn't know and didn't want to know.

"No, I staying home."

"You're a big girl. You can play with other children in school."

"I no like be big," I flatly stated.

She took out the Sears catalog and showed me dresses from the children's section.

"Here, I will sew you all these dresses. Look how pretty. You can wear a new dress every day."

Like mother, like daughter; female vanity kicked in. I was a goner and succumbed to the bribe. I realized my big mistake only after I got on the bus. I felt like a little weed in a field of wildflowers. People were talking and laughing, visiting with each other. No one spoke to me. I couldn't see Sammy. I sat there scared that the bus would take me to Hilo and I would be lost forever. I should have stayed home.

When the bus dropped us off, an older student accompanied Sammy and me to class. I was too scared to admire my new dress and tagged along after Sammy like Mary's little lamb.

That first day of kindergarten came and went. I knew I would not return, and no Sears catalog could make me change my mind. My mother tried everything but failed to get me back on that bus.

After a few weeks, the Sears catalog came out again, and the bribe was larger this time.

"I'll sew you matching schoolbags for each of your dresses. I'll sew you many many new dresses." This time her bribe didn't work; I was, by now, a more experienced five-year-old. I shook my head. All the dresses in the world would not stop policemen from dragging me to jail. I wasn't going, and that was final.

This wasn't the first time I had learned about fear. It had happened with Sammy's father when I was three. I was standing on our front porch when

Sammy's father walked past with a burlap bag slung over his shoulder. He was on his way to the beach.

"I'm going to catch you and put you in my bag," he teased, but I took him seriously and ran into the house.

"I made a big mistake," I heard him tell my parents. "She always runs when she sees me now. We really need to be careful what we say to the children. She's still afraid of me."

Burlap bags and policemen were scary things, always tempting me to hide in the attic for good—that is, if we had had one.

The lures and the bribes continued, but I knew better. The kindergarten teacher sent a note through Sammy: "Please return to school. We miss you."

Sammy dropped by to show me his artwork. "If you come back, you can make dis, too."

"No," I said, sitting on the porch, "I have to stay home. My father miss me." My father cut cane all day long. His five-year-old daughter's absence was of no importance. But that was my answer, and I wouldn't budge.

That Easter, Sammy showed me his Easter basket. It was made out of colored construction paper, filled with artificial grass and multicolored candy eggs. I was filled with envy, but I refused to return to a place where policemen were waiting for me with handcuffs. I didn't need to attend school to learn what they did to children.

"If you not good, I calling the policeman to take you away to jail." It was a standard threat in Sammy's family. His mother used it whenever she needed to discipline him. Not that it did any good in Sammy's case. Sammy never bought into the threat. He continued to get into trouble. Once we played cops and robbers, and Sammy said, "You're the bad guy," and stabbed my sister in her hand with his pocketknife.

Sammy's mother cleaned and bandaged my sister's wound with alcohol, threatening Sammy, "I callin' the police. You goin' jail for this."

It was an idle threat. Never happened, not once. But it took residence in my head. Schoolrooms with policemen in the doorway were no place for five-year-olds with a passionate desire to stay out of jail. I dropped out of kindergarten; the risk wasn't worth a busload of new dresses with matching schoolbags. Not to this Kapoho girl.

THE EMPEROR'S KIDNAPPED DAUGHTER

"I'm here by mistake," I announced. "I was born in Emperor Hirohito's family, and somebody kidnapped me and brought me here."

"Say what you like," my father said. He stood there, watching me use an old broomstick to lift a pair of pants from a large pail of water where the rest of his work clothes were soaking overnight. I transferred a pair of his pants into a cracker barrel filled with very hot water almost to the boiling point over an open fire. "Don't burn yourself," he warned. "We don't want the emperor's daughter to get burned."

The mundane process of laundry day was interrupted by my scream, which could be heard at the outhouse a hundred feet away. The broomstick was on the ground, and a fat reddish-green centipede crawled out of a shirt and scurried down the concrete washtub out of sight. Shivers ran down my spine. *Where are the maids? What am I doing, being scared out of my wits by a centipede? This is no life for an emperor's daughter.*

Brown bubbles and steam rose from the clothes. The pungent odor of sugarcane and sweat filled my nostrils.

Bubbles. Ah, champagne bubbles from a crystal-stemmed glass slip down my throat while the sweet fragrance of rose petals fills the air.

"If you don't get educated," my father interrupted, "you'll end up marrying a plantation worker like me, and you'll be doing this for the rest of your life."

"I'm marrying a rich man and will have maids and butlers," I quipped. "When you visit me in my mansion, my butler will show you in. Be sure to wear a suit and tie."

His laughter followed him to the backyard, and I was left in my prison of drudgery.

I turned the homemade wooden washing board onto its flat surface. I lifted a pair of pants steaming at the end of the broomstick and smoothed one leg of the pants flat on the board. Then I rubbed a bar of soap along the length of the pants leg and scrubbed with a hard bristled brush.

Once the pants were scrubbed, I turned the washboard over onto its corrugated side and worked the pants against the board like a baker kneading dough. Pants were rinsed, wrung out and hung on clotheslines under the hot sun. A big load like today's could take half a day.

The emperor's daughter really has better things to do, I thought, looking down at my hands.

The jagged, broken nails of her red hands become long manicured splashes of crimson color as she walks from one end of the clothesline to the other. Her hands hold a flute instead of wooden clothespins, and the notes from the flute and the trickling of water from a bamboo fountain accompany her through the courtyards of Edo.

On nights when I disregarded my mother's warning to take a bath while it was still light, I sang at the top of my voice to drive away ghosts that might creep into the bathhouse. The kerosene lamp cast strange moving shadows on the wall. I averted my eyes from the window where the faces of ghosts might appear and spoil my song.

"What a beautiful voice." I heard my father's voice interrupt my rendition of "Sentimental Journey." "What a shame to waste such a voice. She belongs in Hollywood."

"Just watch me," I snipped. "Someday I'll be in Hollywood. I'll be riding in a red convertible wearing large sunglasses, with my scarf trailing behind me."

The closest I came to Hollywood was one summer during the sugarcane harvest. Cane was harvested every three years. Every so often, the plantation company changed the regular cane to a different brand that yielded a higher sugar content. This meant that new cane stalks had to be planted between the rows of the old ones. As the new cane stalks began to show their green shoots, the old ones were chopped down. It could take two or three rounds of doing this, working through the entire thirteen acres under the hot, sizzling sun.

That summer at nearby Warm Springs, "Hollywood" filmed the movie *Bird of Paradise*, starring Louis

Jourdan, Debra Paget and Jeff Chandler. For weeks I stood in the hot cane field and watched the caravans of "Hollywood" pass on the long country road. Sometimes, from the distance, I waved and shouted, "Hey, Louis Jourdan!"—glad that he couldn't see the emperor's daughter dressed in denim jeans and old, faded, long-sleeved work shirts.

It didn't help to hear the neighborhood kids brag, "We went down to Warm Springs today. Jeff Chandler came to talk to us. He's really nice and talked story with us."

I wanted to be with the village children instead of under the hot sun doing slave labor. Kapoho was no place for the emperor's daughter and a future Oscar-winning, Pulitzer Prize–winning poet.

I picked up one of my father's left-handed cane knives. It was sharpened on the opposite side of the blade for left-handed users. Hmmm, the emperor must be left-handed, too. With the sun beating down on my body, I chopped each of the old cane shoots down to the ground.

My sister came over to my row. "You need to chop it down real good so they don't grow back again." She showed me how it was done. Her way would be more time-consuming. I couldn't care less about whether they grew again; the sooner I finished, the faster I'd be out of there. Warm Springs and Louis Jourdan's accent were waiting for me. I used my soiled long sleeve to wipe the tears from my face.

Someone had noticed. For the remainder of the summer, whenever I came to the end of a row, the last three feet had already been cut.

Under that hot sun, with sweat sticking my clothes to my body like wet silk and with my muscles aching, lunchtime would be my Hollywood. Every day would be the same script. My oldest brother would peek into the lunch pail and ask, "What do you think we're having for lunch?"

A list of Kapoho cuisine would be shouted out: Spam! Eggs! Vienna sausage! Rice with ume! Tap water in a thermos, champagne for the emperor's daughter.

At the dinner table, after a hard day's work, my father's voice was filled with pride. "Other families hire people to work in their cane fields. We don't need to do that. I'm lucky to have good children."

"Yes, but look at me. I'm stuck in a place that has no electricity or even a water system. We have an outhouse, one battery-run radio, a kerosene stove, not even a pay phone anywhere. We don't even have a car, and Hilo is twenty miles away!"

"I know," my father replied. "I was kidnapped, too." My father's voice faded into the background with the rest of the dinner conversation. Over the sink, doing the dishes later, I belted out one of my favorite songs:

If I should ever travel, to China I would go,
Japan and South Korea, these lands I'd like to know.

The Philippines I'd visit, the Polynesian isles,
Australia and New Zealand, from pole to pole I'd go.

My home is down Pacific, way down Hawai'i nei,
Oh, may our land be peaceful, forever and for aye.

For now, the reality of being kidnapped in Kapoho closed in. My sister was going to give me my first hair perm. She took a large nail between a pair of metal tongs and held it in the fire under the cracker barrel filled with my father's work clothes. She wound sections of my hair around the hot nail and let them sizzle and burn. There was nothing royal about the smell of burnt hair. That night I awoke from a dream that my hair was straight again. I crawled out from under the futon with a flashlight and found a mirror to check on my perm. I still looked like Bette Davis. I returned to bed and dreamed of seeing myself on movie screens.

In my waking hours, I filled empty shoeboxes with poems, stories, favorite book titles, letters and photos. A pen pal from Michigan sent photos of herself sitting in a tree, munching on a red apple. A pen pal from Maryland sent a picture of herself in a strapless white prom gown in front of a television set in her living room. There was a photo of someone skating on a frozen pond. Letters written on onionskin airmail stationery from a pen pal from France were bundled together with a rubber band. Each letter repeated the last, but he was French, which meant Paris would be my next stop.

A postal worker in a Chicago mailroom sent a letter. "I am handicapped from the war. I work from a wheelchair and suffer from a nervous disorder. I am thirty-four years old. I work at the post office, and I often see your letters to Michigan pass through my hands. I've always dreamed of Hawaii. Will you write to me?"

"He's too old" was my first thought. I offered to give his name to one of my female teachers. "Don't you want a more matured woman since I'm only a kid?" He rejected the idea.

Then one day, after months of correspondence, he sent a black-and-white photo of himself. How could a man who wrote such beautiful thoughts in blue script not be handsome like William Holden or Robert Taylor? How could a man who began each letter with "My Dear Frances" not be Hollywood-star handsome? I tore up his photo and stopped writing, but I added all his letters to one of my secret boxes. In a box was a story I wrote in fifth grade:

> *Once upon a time, there lived a girl whose classmates were very wealthy. Every September, on the first day of school, they talked about their summer travels to Paris, New York City and London. The girl listened in envy. The following summer while her friends traveled to all those faraway places, she spent her summer in the public library. When she returned to school in September, she told stories about her travels to Africa, India and Russia. She described each country, her favorite places and their people. She repeated a conversation between a Communist*

and herself in Moscow. No one ever discovered she had never left home.

Determined to fit in at those elegant cocktail parties in New York, Paris and London, the emperor's daughter reads Good Housekeeping, Vogue *and the latest Sears catalog. She keeps up with* Time *magazine's Ten Best Fiction and Nonfiction Books. She studies* The New Yorker's *cartoons and subscribes to* Psychology Today. *She is still using the outhouse but is ready to discuss any book or current event, with a glass of wine held in a hand bedecked with diamond bracelets and rings.*

Later, as a freshman in college, I was working as a live-in maid for room and board when earthquakes and lava flows slowly demolished Kapoho. I was studying for exams. The villagers evacuated with the help of the Red Cross and the National Guard. No one knew about Emperor Hirohito's daughter. My shoeboxes were left behind.

IT WAS ONCE UPON A TIME

"I raised myself" flew out of my mouth more than once after I became the all-knowing college graduate. No one disputed me.

"Say whatever you like," my mother responded. So I did. It was easy to come to this conclusion from all the books I had buried my face in since the day I learned to read.

Parents in novels weren't anything like my own. They conversed with their children at the dinner table, shared the day's events and asked, "How was your day, dear?" They lectured about what was right and wrong and regulated house rules and curfews. Fathers had one-on-one conversations with their daughters about career dreams, while mothers explained the facts of life. They gave weekly allowances, paid their children for chores and went on vacations together. More importantly, parents talked to their children in long paragraphs. That was the true American family. I knew that as a kid. I read about them.

My father was a laborer, a cane cutter working in the fields from dawn to dusk. He spent his evening walking miles to go fishing to put fish on our dinner table.

He often awakened us in the middle of the night. "Wake up, wake up, come and eat mullet. Better to eat fresh." We sat around the dinner table, half asleep, eating slices of raw mullet soaked in shoyu, hot mustard and lemon juice. You didn't see this in movies or in books.

Day after day, my mother sat hunched over her sewing machine, pumping the pedal, making clothes for the villagers. Most of her conversations were with clients who came with Sears and Montgomery Ward catalogs in hand, wanting a replica of the latest fashion. "Stand still. If I measure wrong, you get crooked pants," I often heard from the porch.

After my mother was diagnosed with Alzheimer's, I began to think about my family life. What I found was a silhouette without a face. I was never really there; I was daydreaming, designing life somewhere else, in New York City or Hollywood. As I watched my mother's dying face, I wondered how two parents, with third- and fifth-grade educations, could have started their family as strangers in an arranged marriage and raised five children without the help of Dr. Spock. They taught me without lessons or lectures, and I learned without knowing I was learning. They told stories from their own childhood, from the folklore and myths of their grandparents. Without knowing it, these became the conversations I never had. But I never knew that as a child.

My father, the oldest child, was forced to drop out of third grade to help his mother care for his five younger siblings.

"I had to run over ten miles to go to the store while other children were in school. All I remember are scoldings from my mother; I could never please her. But my stepfather was a nice man."

Years later, when I returned to his bedside as he lay dying from stomach cancer, I saw him as a barefoot nine-year-old boy running long, hot miles on a gravel road to appease his mother, and I wept more for that little boy than for the man who was dying.

I wept for my mother, too. My fingers instinctively curled, as if to grasp a magic wand to return my mother to her youth and to capture something she never had. "You are lucky," she often told her granddaughters. "Grandma never dated and went out with boys. Grandma couldn't choose her own husband. In our days, it was all arranged."

My mother brought to parenting her own manual of child rearing. Spankings were unknown to us, as were reprimands. My sister and brothers and I slept in one room on futons spread out on the floor. We talked late into the night, rehashing a Charlie Chaplin movie or mercilessly impersonating our principal, Mrs. James. Our giggles and laughter bounced off the walls until we heard my father, from the next room, clear his throat. We knew it was a signal to shut up and go to sleep, and we did.

When I wanted cash for candy, or a box of sanitary napkins, my mother's handbag was in the top drawer of her bureau. I took what I needed and told her in passing, "I took some money." Other kids used allowances, and I envied them. Why couldn't I have parents who were more American?

There was an understanding that whatever chores were mine, I would grow into them or they would grow into me. When I was six, I observed my oldest brother building a fire under a wooden tub.

"What you doing?" I asked.

"Making furo fire," he said to my back as I skipped off to some new distraction.

When I was twelve, I hunched on my knees and watched intently as he poured kerosene onto the ashes in the fireplace under the wooden bathtub. Two pieces of firewood were laid about a foot apart on the ashes. Two more were put crosswise on top, and he didn't stop until the pyramid reached almost to the top of the fireplace. He lit a match and threw it on the ashes drenched with kerosene. The fire whooshed and engulfed the firewood. No one told me, but I knew that soon it would be my turn to begin preparing the evening bath.

"I can do that," I said to myself. "Do things fast and easy. Time will fly, and I'll be out of Kapoho before I know it."

One rainy afternoon, I poured kerosene on the wet firewood and watched as the brown bubbles seeped out from the ends. I sat mesmerized, floating away in a gigantic bubble over Kapoho to unknown places. Black smoke stung my eyes and burst my brown bubble. I poured more kerosene, lit a match, threw it on the wet wood and turned away. I had better things to do, returning to the porch and the book I had left facedown on the wooden chair.

After a hard day's work, my father went into the bathhouse, expecting to find a tub of steaming hot water. "The water is cold!" he shouted. "Who made the furo today?" I pretended to be mute and deaf while my brother scurried to restart the fire.

Other times, singed eyebrows and bangs jolted me back to reality. Years later, my younger brother would watch me, and the art of making a furo fire would be passed on.

Coming of age was also just a passage handed down from one child to the next without rites or ceremony. I stood on the concrete floor while my sister soaped me. The tin container that she dipped into the furo disappeared from sight. I prepared my body for the pour of warm water that would fall from above to end this daily ritual. But my mind would never fail to be surprised as the first splashes of the here and now jolted it back from some excursion to the world of wishes.

After getting out of the wooden tub, a brisk toweling and a pat on my butt. A splash on her face for a thank-you, and out the door I ran to the next game.

Some of the lessons were all the more significant for the absence of any instruction. What was said in silence wasn't so easy to merely skip away from. Nothing had to be said when my sister began to bathe alone. Her sexuality was screened with silence, and I knew it was time to stay out of her bath. It was the same when I stopped bathing my younger brothers; they didn't need to know why I stopped. I just did.

Throughout my childhood, there were no daughter-and-parent conversations, but superstitions and myths.

"The kimotori will steal your liver if you're outside after dark. In Japan, children who stay out late are found the next morning without their livers."

"Once in Kapoho," I was further warned, "a child was found near the railroad tracks with her liver missing." The bodies of children with their livers plucked out ran cold in my mind.

It didn't matter if I were in the middle of a favorite game—like kanapio, for instance, the local kids' diversion played like baseball using pieces of wood. The kanapio could be flying through the air, but if the sun were on its last legs, without a word to my friends, I was already halfway home.

The railroad tracks were a dangerous place. "Her body was found by the railroad tracks" was one of the versions of the kimotori stories recounted. In the shadows, beneath the cattle guard of the forbidden crossing, my friend Sammy and I crouched down, listening for the train passing overhead, the hot oil splashing on our heads. A heavy, deep clacking of wheels was a full load of cane being carried to the mill. Other times it would be the tinny rattle of the empty deadhead roaring overhead. But the sound of the sun falling silently below the horizon of cane fields and ʻōhiʻa trees screamed louder than the noisiest locomotive. I was out of there, reaching the front porch and checking the road for strange shadows. Without a thought, my body made the journey in an instant and left Sammy to look out for himself. I had my liver to keep.

When it came to telling lies, George and his cherry tree were child's play next to Ema-san. "When you lie, Ema-san will come and cut off your tongue."

"Lemme see, lemme see. I think Ema-san cut off your tongue!" We exposed many liars among neighborhood kids.

"If you leave your clothes hanging out of the bureau drawers, you will have a difficult childbirth" was all my mother said when she saw me put laundry away with pieces of clothing hanging out of the half-closed drawers. I returned to refold my nightgown and properly close the drawers.

Even today, I take a few seconds to put my clothes back into the drawer. I sometimes walk away with a bra strap hanging out of a drawer, but that voice will return me to the bra strap. It's been decades since my childbearing years, but I still glance back after putting the laundry away. One can't be too careful.

Dinner-table manners took only a few sentences.

"You'll turn into a cow if you slouch at the dinner table." No one's taking me out to the pasture.

"That's the emperor's rice! Your eyes will shut if you waste his rice." The starving Chinese families lived in my books. The emperor's rice was on my table.

The road out of Kapoho was long and seemingly endless. I walked out with my liver and eyesight. In my hands, two scholarships and a live-in maid's job for free room and board, and in my pocket, book stories of perfect families, a handbook for future use. I was ready to design and live that storybook all-American life. After all, didn't I raise myself to do all that? Life ought to be easy and fast out of Kapoho.

"I'm out!" I shouted, but it was the first tiny step out of Kapoho.

TAXI MONEY

She was my mother for sixty-five years. She was my mother and never told me, "I love you," or that she was proud; she never hugged me or held my hand. Instead, up to the time she was diagnosed with Alzheimer's, she gave me taxi money instead.

I spent all my Christmases with her and put up a tree in her living room, and like a yearly playback recording, I would hear her say with childlike delight, "Ah, Christmas is here, now Santa Claus will come. We can't have Christmas without a tree."

What she really meant was that she needed a tree so that she could enjoy her gifts before Christmas. I first learned of how she was taking a peek at all her gifts when I was in high school. I was sitting under the tree one day, to read the names on the gift tags, when I noticed that the ribbons around her gifts were loosely tied and the wrapping on the bottom of each gift was torn and retaped.

"You opened your presents!" I accused. "You're terrible."

"Shhh," she laughed. "Put them back."

"I'm going to open mine, too," I said. And we became two conspirators, adding a new private tradition to our Christmas.

I never caught her at it when she was carrying out her raids, and she never caught me. We'd accuse each other of being sneaky and bad, and before long, the rest of the family called us "worse than children," two adults unable to wait until Christmas. In later years, they gave us our gifts on Christmas Day, but we had other gifts to rifle.

One Christmas, I added another ritual to our tradition when I conned my mother into giving me the gift of my choice.

"Look at this dress I bought today. Do you want to give this to me for Christmas?"

"You can't buy your own clothes with all the money you make?"

"I'm doing you a favor. This way, you don't need to worry about what to get me for Christmas."

Her comments were always the same as she handed me cash for the cost of my gift.

"You not shame to take money from your poor mother?"

She's been gone since 2002, and I still purchase an extravagant gift from her every Christmas, and I still open my gifts as soon as they arrive.

"What if I die tonight?" I explain to the next generation of nieces and nephews. "I don't want to die not knowing what was in the gift. How sad is that?"

My visits home to my mother's house in Pāhoa ended on the back steps. I would have my carry-on and handbag in hand, ready to leave for the airport. But we would share one more ritual. My mother would hand me a hundred-dollar bill, saying, "Take care. Here's taxi money."

She knew I had a ride from the airport to my apartment, but she'd press the taxi money into my hand. She had been working on a flower farm since my father's death in 1963, seven days a week, holidays included. It was hard work, I knew. She left the house before sunup to catch a ride to the orchid farm. She wore a hat and a white towel over her head and half her face to protect her from the hot sun, and she began her day by picking vanda orchids from plants that were often too high for her to reach. Once the other pickers brought in their first pick, she became the one-person assembly line, weighing and boxing the orchids to keep up with the flower pickers. At the end of each day, she helped deliver the orchids to Hilo. At home, her labor continued: she raised and sold anthuriums, red ginger flowers, tangerines and navel oranges from her three-acre lot.

"My play money," she'd say. "Otherwise, I starve"—a slight exaggeration.

I earned more money than she did, but no matter how many times she handed me her money, I always took it and said, "Ohhh...taxi money! Thank you." She'd chuckle as I walked down the stairs and waved goodbye, taking her money.

At the airport, I observed a friend hugging her mother. I envied them their intimate moment. I wish I could have done that; I knew my mother would have been delighted, because I'd seen her responses when my nieces and nephews gave her a hug or a kiss, but I was stuck in my upbringing and found it awkward and uncomfortable to break out of that mode.

In later years, there was that taxi money and sometimes a cup of coffee in bed.

For me, mornings were as thick as spilled molasses. In high school I thought of becoming a bank teller, since banks opened after nine, or a waitress who only served lunch and dinner. But after I graduated, I had to put my dreams of sleeping through the mornings on hold, as I became a teacher, living at home the first few years.

On cold winter mornings, I clung deep beneath the covers, beginning with my shouts that echoed through the nearly empty house.

"Somebody! Bring me a cup of coffee! I'm too cold to get up!" Soon footsteps would come from the kitchen.

"Here, you big baby. You not shame to have your poor mother bring you coffee in bed? Better get up. You don't want to speed and get into an accident."

"Would you brush my teeth and wash my face, too?"

Years later, I was living in Honolulu and had a cholecystectomy. My mother flew over and sat all day at my hospital bedside, day after day after day. On the day after surgery, I caught her laughing as she helped me into my new pink robe and matching bedroom slippers.

"What's so funny?" I asked.

She covered her mouth with her hands and tried to stifle her laughter. "I thought only people going on honeymoon bought matching new robe and slippers. This is the hospital, you know."

"You can never tell. Did you get to see the doctor? He looks like a movie star. Don't you want a doctor for a son-in-law?" I held my stitches as I laughed.

Five days later, we went back to my small studio apartment, where we shared the sofa bed and had our meals in my dollhouse of a kitchenette.

"So this is how city people live" was her only comment. We flew back to her home on the Big Island, where I convalesced for the next six weeks. It was a place where birds woke me in the morning and flowers sent their fragrances through the front door, which stayed open during the day and remained unlocked at night. The kitchen was big enough for five couples to waltz and dip. It was a place for deep breathing and healing.

For the next twenty-two years, I lived in Honolulu and returned home to celebrate our traditional Christmas. Then Alzheimer's crept into our lives and changed everything.

She lived the last years of her life with me in Honolulu, and a new ritual was created: every Saturday, I walked with her at the mall after her hair appointment.

"We're going to the hairdresser" became magical words to speed our mornings. On weekdays, she was prodded and nudged to get dressed for adult day care, but "hairdresser" had her ready within minutes.

For the first time, I held her hand. It was as though we had been holding hands forever. I could feel her ring press into mine. I squeezed her hand, and she chuckled. It was like passing taxi money.

"Look at that." A teenager who was walking through the mall with his friends pointed at us. "Just look at that. That is so awesome. When I'm old, I want my wife or my kid to hold my hand and walk me around the mall like that." His teenage friends were silent. From the looks on their faces, I could almost read, *"So what's the big deal about holding hands?"*

During the last year of her disease, she didn't recognize me. I hugged her. I massaged her legs and arms. I kissed her forehead. Her speech was gone. My name was gone. Why did I wait so long? Perhaps I waited until her mind was no longer there so that I could finally hug her and show her physical affection without disrespecting and defying that dance we had danced throughout her life. Or was it my dance alone? Silence had always ruled us when it came to expressing our feelings, and I had to believe that she knew that this was the last gesture left for me when language and recognition were no longer available. There were no Christmas gifts to peek into, no walks in the mall, no funny bantering between mother and daughter, not even a chuckle or a cup of hot coffee in bed. All we had between us was a little taxi money.

A KAPOHO CHRISTMAS

It was Christmas without lights.
It was Christmas without indoor plumbing.
It was Christmas without carolers at the window
Muffed and warm under falling snow.

But there was Christmas.
A Christmas program at school
The Holy Night reenacted:
White tissue paper glued on spines of coconut fronds
Shaped as angel wings and halos.
Long white robes, over bare feet.

The plantation manager with bagfuls of assorted hard candies
His annual role in the village where he reigned.
Fathers in Sunday best
After a hard day's work in sugarcane fields.
Mothers in dresses fashioned after the Sears catalog.
Children, restless, on wooden benches,
Waiting for Santa's jolly Ho Ho Ho.

A fir tree from the hills,
Needles not lasting 24 hours.
Chains from construction paper,
Origami balls and strands of tin-foiled tinsel.
Kerosene and gas lamps
Moving shadows on the walls.

It was not the Christmas of my dreams.
No carolers at the window,
Singing "Silent Night, Holy Night."
No large presents under a real Christmas tree.
No fireplaces and rooftop chimneys.
No blue-eyed boy handing me hot chocolate.

For 18 years, the true Christmas
Lived in my head until Madame Pele
Came to my rescue
And buried our kerosene lamps.

"Finally!" I said, without a backward glance,
Running out fast in bare feet
On unpaved roads
To the Christmas of my dreams.

MRS. HONDA'S BEAUTIFUL DAUGHTER

When Mrs. Honda died, one of my two faces was buried with her.

It's a mystery how messages were received in small plantation villages where there were no private telephones, local newsletters or community bulletin boards. In Kapoho, a village of fewer than a thousand people, the following message from the plantation hospital was delivered to every household where a five-year-old lived:

"All children entering first grade should have their tonsils removed by Dr. McKenzie."

Even at five years old, I was suspicious of the hospital and Dr. McKenzie. They called him "Horse Doctor." No matter what the symptoms, when villagers went to his office, they walked out with the same pills. Soon they would share them with other family members. It saved more trips to the hospital.

Horse Doctor or not, he was the only doctor available, unless my parents borrowed someone's car to drive us to a private doctor in Hilo. Even so, city doctors were viewed with some suspicion. And besides, Horse Doctor was cheaper.

When my ten-year-old sister complained of a severe stomachache, my parents decided that this was too serious for the plantation doctor and took her to Hilo. Within minutes the physician made his diagnosis: "It's her appendix; it needs to come out today."

My mother thanked him, hurried my sister out of the office and took her to Mrs. Yamada, the village midwife and witch doctor. Mrs. Yamada had been there when my mother's water broke and my brother was coming out feet first. Mrs. Yamada had magic in her hands; a little massage, and my brother turned and came out right side up. That was why my mother took my sister to Mrs. Yamada that day.

"No, no," Mrs. Yamada said, after pressing my sister's stomach. "No need for surgery. Yaito will fix this." She marked a spot on my sister's arm and instructed, "Burn six yaito three times a day on this spot until pain is gone."

Yaito was a simple remedy, though extremely painful. Mugwort herbs called moxa, aged and ground into a fluff like lint from a dryer, were a staple in most Japanese medicine cabinets. My mother placed a pearl-sized fluff of moxa on the spot marked on my sister's arm and lit it. A tiny flame engulfed the moxa and burned itself out. She repeated this six times. My sister did not even whimper. After all, being burned was better than having someone cut your stomach open. She had no problem with her appendix after the yaito treatment, though she still bears a burn scar to this day.

For cuts and bruises and other ailments, we would go to our neighbor Nalani for her Native Hawaiian medicine. For diarrhea, we chewed the young leaves of the guava plant and swallowed the bitter juice. For cuts and scrapes, we chewed the young shoots, then applied them to the open wounds to stop the bleeding. Squatting over the steam of burning fig leaves cured hemorrhoids, and a piece of aloe worked as well as a suppository.

One day, my father fell off the roof and lost consciousness for a few minutes. Nalani gave him a cup of warm water mixed with Hawaiian sea salt. He recovered completely.

But when the message about tonsillectomies buzzed around the village, we all paid attention. Horse Doctor or not, Dr. McKenzie was still the voice of medical authority, so I was on his waiting list, too, along with other five-year-olds in Kapoho.

Mrs. Honda, one of the mothers in the village, placed even greater faith in doctors, or anyone with a title before his or her name. She scheduled her daughter Hiroko to be the first to have her tonsils out that summer.

News of Hiroko's surgery traveled rapidly. There would be no other tonsillectomy that year. Hiroko died on the operating table. Horse Doctor had overdosed her with ether. Needless to say, I still have my tonsils today.

The villagers, dressed in black suits and dresses, showed up for Hiroko's funeral service at the Honda home. Hiroko's casket was surrounded by orchids and azaleas from people's yards. The scent of incense and the soft Buddhist sutra from the priest greeted me when I entered the room with my mother. Imitating my mother, I went up to the Buddhist shrine next to the casket, lit a stick of incense and placed it upright in the incense urn with all the others. I put my hands together in prayer, with my own rosary called o-juzu around both my hands, and followed my mother to Mrs. Honda.

Mrs. Honda was weeping, "What shall I do? What shall I do?" to everyone who offered condolences. No one had an answer. Hiroko had been her youngest child. Hiroko was irreplaceable. Mrs. Honda was inconsolable.

When it was my turn, Mrs. Honda reached out and touched my face.

"Hiroko, Hiroko, *honto ni kawai*, truly precious, so beautiful." Before I could say anything, someone pulled on my skirt and hurried me along. But it was too late. In that brief moment, I became two daughters.

A few months later, I passed Mrs. Honda on the way to the store. She stared at me and then began to weep and said, "If Hiroko were alive, she would look like you." I stared back at her without saying a word.

During my teens, whenever we met, Mrs. Honda would look at my face and say, "What a beautiful face. Hiroko would look exactly like you." In those years, I looked like a photo on a CARE package, in loosely fitted homemade dresses and a haircut styled by my father's scissors. Mrs. Honda never noticed. She'd say, "Just look at your flawless complexion." She was mercifully blind to my freckles and pimples, my small "single-eyes" and skinny body. My family teased me each time I ran home bragging, "I saw Mrs. Honda, and she said I was beautiful."

"Yeah," my brother Paul laughed, "just like a morning glory, all dried up at the end of the day." To this day, Paul still calls me "MG."

Mrs. Honda worked as a laborer in the cane fields. Whenever I saw her in her work clothes, with a towel covering half her face to protect it from the sun, she was full of apologies and embarrassed to have me see her in her oversized, long-sleeved denim shirt, her pants tied at the waist with a cord. On her feet were denim Japanese tabi with rubber soles.

"Look at me in these work clothes," she'd say. "Look at my face, so dark and ugly. But look at you. Your face is so beautiful. Hiroko would look like you today."

I accepted her compliments with a smile. Mrs. Honda had just outshouted the boys in the hallway, the same boys who hid *Playboy* under their mattresses, the ones who whispered, "Eh, Stew Bones," as I passed by, clutching my oversized jacket to my chest.

To have discounted this compliment, even from a naïve and simple woman, would have denied Mrs. Honda her image of Hiroko and would have denied Stew Bones the confidence to take off her jacket. I wonder if Mrs. Honda knew what a lift she gave me that day.

Mrs. Honda also extended her family by one other member: my father. He occasionally worked with Mr. Honda on the papaya farm after his retirement from the sugar plantation. One day, he returned home from work saying, "That silly woman. Today she packed a lunch for me, too."

"Ohhh," I teased, "she has a crush on you."

We all knew that Mrs. Honda checked the work schedule, and on days when Mr. Honda and my father worked together, she would pack fancy lunches with food usually reserved for New Year's Day: sushi, shrimp tempura and nishime.

"Look at that bakatare woman," Mr. Honda would say. "I don't know what got into her." And then he'd spread her lunch for the two of them. Mr. Honda allowed Mrs. Honda these simple pleasures, chalking them up to his wife's continuing grief.

Whenever I saw Mrs. Honda going past our house with her head down, I'd call out to my father, "Come quick. Come quick. Your girlfriend is passing." I could tell that Mrs. Honda didn't want to be noticed in her dirty work clothes.

My father would chuckle, "You can say whatever you like."

When my father died, Mrs. Honda was the first to arrive from the neighborhood to offer her condolences. She openly wept and called out my father's name. I was older then and held her to me. We hugged each other as if we'd always been doing that.

A few weeks before my high school graduation, my photo appeared in the *Hilo Tribune-Herald* because of a scholarship that I had received. The next day, Mrs. Honda stopped me on the roadside and said, "If Hiroko were alive, she'd be just like you. Smart and beautiful."

In Mrs. Honda's eyes, Hiroko accompanied me to college, and we both became teachers. After graduating from college, I didn't see much of Mrs. Honda in Kapoho, but when I did, she would always say, "Hiroko would have become a teacher just like you."

On one occasion, she said, "How lucky you have a tall nose, just like a haole. Look at your white complexion, just like a haole. You are truly beautiful." I was a college graduate, a grown woman, but still I had the urge to return home to tell the family, "Mrs. Honda still thinks I'm beautiful."

When my first four books were published, Mrs. Honda attended each of my book signings. Though she was issei like my grandmothers and had never learned to read or write in Japanese or English, she bought my books, held them in both hands and bowed.

Why she chose me among all the girls in the village I will never know. But to Mrs. Honda, the child who became her surrogate daughter was the most beautiful child in Kapoho. Her face glowed with love and affection when she looked at me, and I accepted her praises with a smile.

When Hiroko had died, there were whispers in the village that it could have been a blessing. "She would have struggled in school," people said. They did not believe that Hiroko could ever have become an independent adult or have met someone someday who would have accepted her as his wife. Children had teased Hiroko. They called her "Mochi Face," as they once called me "Stew Bones."

Someday when my face turns into a wadi bed, my skin is mottled with dark liver spots and my hair is sparse and gray, I want to hear Mrs. Honda saying once more, "Hideko-san, you are beautiful."

THERE WAS A MAN NAMED DAVI

I sat in terror in Professor Davi's basic music class at the University of Hawai'i. I was the only one with panic showing on her face. I looked at the others sitting around me and saw them nodding in agreement. Kapoho had failed me once again, even before the first class hour was over.

My mother never liked one story that I retold often as an adult. Why would I repeat a story she found unpleasant? Was I implying that she had failed me as a parent by not getting me a violin? One day by pure accident I heard a violin sonata pouring out of our battery-powered radio. Violin music rarely rode the airwaves into our house, but when it did I was so entranced I knew I wanted a violin in my hand. I found a broomstick, sawed it off to violin length, put it under my chin and pretended I was the violinist. I played my "violin" constantly in the living room. Now that was pretty easy, moving the imaginary bow across the shortened broomstick under my chin, swaying in time to the music. Soon I didn't need the radio; I played the broomstick with the music pouring out of my head.

My sister had something better going for her. She took piano lessons in Hilo and practiced on imaginary keys. Her fingers flew over those invisible keys, pausing when she made an error or stumbled over some notes. She was always ready for her next lesson in Hilo and later was allowed to use the piano in the community hall for an hour a day. I continued to play my broomstick.

Professor Davi's voice was barely audible above the anxious pounding in my chest. "The finals," he said, "will be pretty standard." He waved a blank music sheet at us and continued, "I'll play a few chords on the piano and all you'll need to do is fill in the notes on a sheet like this."

It was back to the cane fields for me. How was I going to pass this basic music course to earn my teaching diploma? It was a requirement. Ellen and Ella, both Hilo High graduates, wore calmness on their faces—they'd both had years of piano lessons since childhood. I knew nothing about musical notations. How was listening to Arthur Godfrey and his 'ukulele going to help me now? I sang in the chorus in high school; that was it. As for instruments, there was only my broomstick violin. See why I needed to get out of Kapoho? Madame Pele, you came too late. Look at me now. What am I going to do?

I never knew that fear could manifest itself as physical pain in my gut and shorten my breath to gasping. I wanted to forget my dreams and go home.

Professor Davi was the epitome of a music professor, with his white hair curled against the nape of his neck, his handlebar moustache waxed and perfectly pointed. He seemed pleased with the image he produced for his young, naïve students.

I attended class for a few weeks, feeling like an alien. I took no notes and merely listened, hating every moment in class, knowing I was failing. Then one night, alone in my room where I worked as a live-in maid, my Kapoho survival instinct kicked in.

A few classes later, out of pure desperation—a swimmer going under and gulping for air, a mountain climber slipping down a slick icy slope, a fish out of water gasping for breath—I introduced Plan A. I went to class early and left a handwritten poem on Professor Davi's desk. A few minutes later I watched his face as he read the poem and saw a glint of pleasure flash across his face. He was ready for Plan B.

About a week after that, I stood up in class before he could begin and announced, "Professor, I wrote you a poem and I'd like to read it." I had been carrying it in my handbag for weeks. It was now or never.

Sometimes, the planets will be perfectly aligned, and the gods will begin their day with kindness in their hearts for the desperate and the scared. The class applauded after I read the poem, and Mr. Davi even asked for a copy. From the look on his face, I knew I had a fifty-fifty chance of passing his course and it wasn't going to be through his piano.

I wrote him poems throughout the semester. Now and then I would read them in class, but most of them

I just left on his desk. Once I daringly left a long-stemmed red rose with my poem, much to his delight.

The finals were just as he had explained on the first day of class. He passed out blank music sheets, went to the piano and played a few chords. I watched Ella and Ellen fill their lines with notes, as did the rest of the class. I sat and trembled, too terrified to even think of copying my neighbor's notes. Russian poets, I once read, were considered more powerful than the KGB. "Oh, please let my pen be as powerful," I prayed. I handed in a blank sheet, folded over twice.

On the last day of class, Professor Davi followed me out and said, "I need to speak to you." *Oh, shit,* I thought. *Please, God, let me pass.*

He took both my hands in his and said, "You make me feel I was born too soon."

I giggled and walked away, for I was only eighteen years old. I received an A for the course and was on my way to a college degree. Or so I thought, until I took Speech 100 and felt the same terror of failure all over again.

Fifty-six years later, I was signing books at a bookshop in Honolulu. I sensed someone standing near me and before I could look up, I heard a woman's voice reciting:

> There was a man named Davi
> Whose hair was white and wavy.
> But when his fingers hit the ivories
> There was music smoother than gravy.

"I was in Mr. Davi's class with you," said the woman. "I never forgot you or the poem you read in class. I always admired you and thought you were someone so special, so independent and confident."

I signed her copy of *Kapoho: Memoir of a Modern Pompeii* and briefly thought of that frightened eighteen-year-old as I handed the book back to her.

THE UNFINISHED DANCE

We should not have started the dance. But we did. He was the one with pain in his eyes.

There was nothing I couldn't do that weekend. Published twice with two books of poetry, I had given myself a writer's weekend on Molokaʻi. I was going to live like a writer, out of my cultural webs, free and daring. I walked into the hotel with my portable typewriter and a thin collection of poetry that I planned to build into a full manuscript. Before I could even unpack, "She's a writer" buzzed around the hotel. "Your typewriter," one of the maids explained. "Only writers come here with typewriters."

I spent the first evening poolside with my antennae fully extended, hoping to glean a poem or two from the cool summer evening. The ink was flowing, the pool was surrounded by men on R&R from Vietnam. The moon was full and soft chatter filled the air.

The Molokaʻi Trio, with ʻukuleles in hand, approached me. "Come dance 'My Yellow Ginger Lei' again?"

Scotch and water over ice had prompted my first dance an hour earlier in the dining room. The trio moved from table to table, serenading diners with their Hawaiian melodies. I sipped my scotch and water, and when they reached my table, they asked if I had a request.

"Do you know 'My Yellow Ginger Lei'?"

They sang the first line in harmony. I boldly asked, "Can I dance?"

I took the outstretched hand—I'll blame it on the scotch—stood and danced hula as they sang and strummed. We stopped diners' forks in midair; it was a tourist's delight.

"Dance another one!" they said.

I whispered sheepishly, "I only know 'My Yellow Ginger Lei.'"

Beside the pool now, they didn't need to ask twice. With the lingering effects of the scotch and a half-written poem bolstering my courage, we became the Moloka'i Quartet. I danced around the pool under romantic tiki torch flares casting flickering shadows upon us. The men on R&R applauded, appearing happy with drinks and song. Except for one. He was the one with pain in his eyes.

"You're the writer," he said later.

"Yes," I answered. "Tell me about Vietnam." I shouldn't have asked.

A helicopter pilot, he had one mission, always the same: to fly in and search for child survivors among the villagers who lay dead or dying in the wake of our American bombs. Each flight had room for only a few children. Forced to play God, he walked among the dead and wounded, selecting the children who seemed the most alive for another chance at life. Did he hear a whimper? Did that child move? He gathered what life he could find and flew the broken bodies back to the field hospital, a mission never really accomplished.

He preserved what he saw, what he did, with a brush and oil paints. He painted the children as wooden logs, splattered red, on canvas after canvas, his own despair hidden beneath each deliberate brushstroke. There were no words yet invented for what he felt.

A week before his R&R, after many such missions, he looked for his canvases and paint, only to find them being tossed into a bonfire by his superiors. "You can't take these home," they said. "The war stays here." The wooden logs on canvas burned to ash, but the scent of burning flesh would follow him home and cling to him for the rest of his life.

It was a story for poets.

Three days later, now back in my studio apartment in Honolulu, his stories continued over cups of tea. He told them to me with his hand grasped around my blue and white teacup, like those children clinging to life. The aroma of green tea failed to diffuse the agony in his voice. I put my hand over his. We would never be the same.

His body shook, going off the Richter scale. I was young, a Zelda, a Sylvia, a poet, believing I could help conquer anything with poetry and love if he stayed. But he was wiser. He would write in his journal later:

I was drawn to her soft voice, her eager searching words. She drew me out of my defensive shell, I told her of the boring hours interspersed with moments of terror. The words didn't come easily; the memories were still too fresh in my mind but I found myself unable to stop and with each word I became more depressed, more agitated. I told her of the Navy Seals, how they made jokes about the body parts. She let me go on, her eyes never leaving my face. My hurt became her hurt. I could not stop. I'd found someone to help me release the demons in myself.

I wanted to stay and never leave. What a quandary I found myself in.

I knew this demon in me would cause her great harm.

"Stay," I wanted to say, but I let it dissipate into silence like the steam from our teacups.

He returned to his home in Virginia, promising he'd be back. He wrote with sharpened pencils, each word etched on paper, with caution and passion. He called me Darling. I was the brilliant, powerful femme fatale poet.

I replied with fountain pens wet with ink, becoming Elizabeth Barrett Browning, Emily Dickinson, Sylvia Plath. I wrote him a poem called "The Wooden Soldier."

The Wooden Soldier

*The wooden soldier marches
As he was wound to do.
Steadily, rhythmically,
Mechanical precision.*

*The only dislocation
Between manufactured knees.
The wooden soldier marches
Then stands perfectly still,
A soldier no more
But a wooden peg.*

*But the soldier I know
Keeps on marching.
He keeps on beating*

*For he has no key
To stop him from seeing
Dislocated limbs
Of children on children.*

*He has no key
To stop him from smelling
The river of blood
On Sunday afternoons.*

*Forgive us, O Soldier
For factorizing keys
Only for soldiers
On wooden knees.*

Forgive us, Soldier,
For mechanized birds,
Wooden logs and battlefields.

It was a time for love, for poetry that begged to be written, rapidly, urgently, before the previous one was finished. He sketched a wooden soldier holding a small injured child—to be painted someday.

Then, like the sharp cracking sound of lightning, shattering windows, like a giant wave knocking me over, filling my lungs with the sea, his letter arrived:

Do not write anymore. This is it. It's all over.
Forgive me, it's all over. Do not write.

I disobeyed. I wrote and wrote, poem after poem, but I never sent them. They, with "The Wooden Soldier," were read by everyone else nine months later in my third book of poetry, *Golden Spike*.

Defiantly determined to have the last word, I also included one of his poems. I dedicated the book to "Someone I Know" and sent him a copy. Many of the poems in *Golden Spike* resonated with war veterans and trauma survivors.

I saved the unpublished poems in a shoebox labeled PRIVATE: penetrating arrows, razor sharp, tearing through cardboard, bleeding red; poetry destructive as warplanes over villages. Red ink dripped from the tip of my pen, long after the last word was written. With time the red faded, and the shoebox remained an attic for old memories.

Thirty-three years passed, and I received a letter from New York, forwarded by my publisher. I recognized the penciled handwriting immediately.

> *I wandered into Borders in Syracuse. I must tell you, you've never, never been far from my thoughts. I was poking through the poetry area, always wondering if, hoping you might, have published another book after* Golden Spike. *Much to my delight, like a punch in the stomach, there was your book,* Mosaic Moon. *I debated for weeks, should I? Why not?*
>
> *I'm sorry but I had to let you go because I was going down and couldn't take you with me. I returned from Vietnam, damaged, one of the forgotten men. PTSD was not invented yet so all the help I got were shrugs and sleeping drugs. Helpless, I had nowhere to turn so I saved all my drugs and at that very moment of ending my life, I heard your voice, intruding into my thoughts… in spite of my anger—my effort to push you aside to seek the comfort of nothingness, your voice became louder and louder. I believe it was my love for you. I have no other words for what pulled me back from the brink of self-destruction.*
>
> *I would have destroyed you. It was the hardest thing I ever had to do when I ended it. I was having frightening dreams, ducked at sudden sounds. I stayed awake to prevent the dreams. I slept with women to ease the memories; almost*

caused the death of one. A helicopter was receiving hostile fire. I was going into a hot landing and the damned thing refused to respond to UP Collective. The landing was rough. The bird began to roll over—I leapt out of bed, shouting and screaming—pulling a crew member out of the burning chopper. I woke up with my hands around the throat of a woman in bed with me. I had to let you go to protect you.

I still have dreams but they live in the shadows now. The instinctive ducking at loud noises comes less and less. Molokai is alive as ever.

Still too poetically naïve, still Sylvia and Zelda, I wrote, "I would have glued all the pieces together." I wasn't young anymore, and he was still wiser.

A few phone calls and emails later, like circling vultures waiting for death, his old message appeared:

I'm sorry. Don't get in touch anymore. Until I lay Molokai and Vietnam to rest, I need peace, peace without you. This is hard to write—I am angry with you for patiently letting me open up the war, coming to terms to what I need to do. Damn you, I can no longer accept shrugs and sleeping drugs from the VA. I need an overhaul of myself and I need to do this without you.

His penciled words have faded once again. "Someday," he said, before his final goodbye, "write our story." This, I could do.

YOU LOOK LIKE, YOU LOOK LIKE…

"Is it difficult being a woman?" the reporter asked.

"No, it's difficult being a *Japanese* woman," I replied. Had there been a follow-up—"Why is that?"—the interview might have gone on a good deal longer. There wasn't any.

In 1961 I was in Ohio, as a guest of my pen pal, Leatrice. She was the mother of my brother's elementary school pen pal, though the boys had only corresponded for a few months. Leatrice sent a letter to our Kapoho address after seeing the story of the eruption in *Life* magazine. "Please," she had written, "please tell me you are all right." The letter found its way to our post-evacuation address. I responded, and we became pen pals.

We met for the first time when I drove to Columbus from Michigan where I was teaching. The local papers printed our story with photos on the front page: *Hawaii Pen Pal Finally Meets Pen Pal In Ohio*.

When I arrived, her living room was filled with relatives and friends eager to meet me. But as they told me about life in Columbus, I heard the N-word repeated over and over. Finally I interrupted the conversation to ask, "If you feel so strongly about color, why am I here? I'm not white." Leatrice answered, "Oh, but you're not black."

I thought I learned something that day, that there was no way to be selectively racist. Those people tried to talk me into sharing their racism for another group as if it wasn't about me. The ugly revelation that day was that racism is here to stay. Just as I could not persuade them to reconsider their attitude and beliefs, neither could they change my opposing views. Once a racist, always a racist, I thought—until children both in and out of my classrooms taught me otherwise later on. Leatrice and her friends were so wrong to assume that only black people could—and should—be discriminated against. The fact is, discrimination comes in many shapes and shades.

In the early 1970s, a friend picked me up at the Maui airport and drove me to her friends' home for dinner. I knew as soon as we arrived that our hosts hadn't expected to see someone wearing my face. As the evening progressed, no one made eye contact with me. Conversations ignored me. I began to feel invisible. A bell was rung for the maid to serve coffee, and afterward I followed her into the kitchen. *Okay, folks,* I thought, *you think I belong in the kitchen with your maid, so that's where I will go.* The Swedish maid and I drank coffee and chatted about her life, while apparently no one missed me in the living room. This was my first encounter with discrimination in my adult life.

Years later, as I stood in a department store checkout line, I observed the woman in front of me, who had coupons and questions about her purchases but never made eye contact with the cashier. She stared past her as though she didn't exist. The cashier was black. After the woman paid and walked away, I made a comment about her rude behavior.

"I get that all the time," the cashier replied. "I'm used to it."

Walking out, I noticed the Less-Than-10-Items checkout counter and imagined another sign reading, *For Racists Only. Cashier is White!*

Soon after I moved to Sacramento, I was in another line, this time in a candy shop behind two white male customers. As soon as the cashier saw me, she asked in a toneless voice if I had cut in line. I looked back and saw no one behind me. I said no.

"Why did you ask me if I cut in line? You didn't ask these two in front of me." At that point, all the customers in the shop froze in silence to listen to our conversation. The cashier ignored me.

"I'd like to know why you asked if I'd cut in line?" I persisted. After a few seconds, the cashier mumbled, "I saw other people looking at you."

"So if someone looks at me, it means I'm cutting in line?" I asked. "Do you ask everyone the same question?"

The cashier was silent. I looked directly at her and slowly said in a loud and firm voice, "I am very sorry that I caused such problems for you." I paid for my purchase and walked out. I had learned by then not to simply escape into kitchens.

My first book of poetry was released in Hawai'i in 1979, when it was less common for anyone, let alone a woman of Japanese ancestry, to publish poetry. A Japanese-American district judge was heard to say, "No Japanese man will ever date her now. She has stepped into the haole world with this book." Overnight, I became known as a "banana"—yellow outside, white inside—but his prediction was accurate. I have yet to be asked out by a Japanese man.

Guilty As Charged

"Did your husband write all these books?"
He was in the audience a few minutes ago.
Yet, here he stands in his three-piece designer suit
Scanning book titles with furrowed brows.

"Idiot," I didn't say, "would I be sitting here,
Two hours on my hemorrhoids
Signing someone else's books
With carpal tunneled fingers?"

At Barnes & Noble in Hawai'i,
The FBI disguised in a loud aloha shirt,
A wilted orchid lei, a camera strapped like a gun
Interrogates me.

"You wrote these books?"
Not satisfied, he grills me over hot coals again.
"You? You wrote all these books?"

Ready to turn the lamp on me,
He turns to his partner.
"Martha? Martha? Come on over.
She said she wrote all these books!"
Expecting the click of handcuffs,
Waterboarding or worse,
I remain silent.

A man in his black robe
Sits on the Court bench.
The Advertiser *news story of my poetry book*
Spread across his lap.
"A Japanese woman publishing poetry…
No Japanese man," he prophesized,
"Is ever going to date her.
She crossed over into the haole world
With this poetry book."

Yes, Your Honor.
Japanese. Woman. Poet.
Guilty as charged.

In my Michigan first grade classroom, I often heard students fire N-words at students of color like dodgeballs. How did I discuss discrimination with six-year-olds? I used my old standby story, *The Boy with Green Hair*. We first separated the children by hair color. The children with red hair put up the chairs for everyone before going home each day. The ones with black hair cleaned the chalkboards. The blonds were free of chores. After a few weeks of assigning chores by hair color, I heard genuine anger and comments of "It's not fair!" It was an effective lesson, one that even first graders could understand.

After a few weeks, a parent stopped by to say, "Thank you for showing my family how careless we have been in using the N-word. Susan pointed this out to us a few nights ago at the dinner table. Last night she told my mother the story of the boy with green hair. Mom wasn't too happy being lectured by her six-year-old granddaughter. I need to warn you, my mother may come in and attack you for teaching about racism. She was plenty mad." The grandmother never did stop by.

There are so many opportunities in our classrooms to stop racism, discriminatory attitudes and behavior before they take hold. After a museum field trip, I heard some of my third graders laughing and making fun of a person with disabilities, who was wiping tables at McDonald's. Back at school, I told the class how disappointed I felt watching them make fun of someone who could have been my nephew, who also works at a McDonald's. A few weeks later, a student came up to my desk to say, "I think I saw your nephew Saturday. We had lunch at McDonald's. I smiled and told him hello." She was one of the students who had snickered at the worker on the field trip. Her mother later told me her daughter had insisted on going to McDonald's for lunch. I shared the incident with her.

For seven years, I taught the sixth grade students of non-commissioned military officers. As December 7 and the anniversary of the attack on Pearl Harbor approached, one of my students, Jason, wrote in his journal, "I hate the Japs. My grandpa told me all about the Japs. I hate them!"

I cringed, but I was the teacher. To challenge Jason's prejudice, I decided to set our social studies textbook aside. Instead I asked each student to choose a country to research. An international luncheon, with food from each student's country of study, would be the project's culmination. Jason, however, was not given a choice. I asked him to research Japan.

"But I hate the Japs," he said.

"I know, Jason. But you know what they say: Sometimes you can weaken the enemy by getting to know how he feels and thinks." He accepted that. His research progressed and his journal entries began to change in tone. I knew why we teach when I read, "I no longer hate the Japanese. They are very much like us."

"Do you know any Japanese I can interview for my project?" he asked one day.

"Me!" I said.

"You?" he replied. As Jason's interview proceeded, he discovered that my ancestors had been killed in the bombing of Hiroshima. At the luncheon, his mother brought a tray of Japanese food, which she had helped research with Jason. He would never know how I had walked to school with my head down after December

7, 1941, with shouts of "Hey, Jap!" echoing behind me. Nor would he know how my heart ached when I'd first read his earlier journal entries.

During my years of teaching, I was always conscious of the power of my voice as a teacher. My passion could so easily affect my students' attitudes and behavior. It didn't always have to do with discrimination. During the latter part of my career, I invited student teachers into my class. That meant leaving the class in their care for their solo teaching. One year, a colleague overheard my student teacher shouting a string of expletives at my sixth graders.

"You better not use that kind of language," one student told him. "Our teacher loves language—in here, language is beautiful."

"Yeah," said another. "You better not swear or you're not going to pass." It wasn't specifically about discrimination or racism, but about how we talk to one another. I took pride in the fact that my students seemed to understand that lesson.

How might a truckload of Marines, a class of first graders and a teacher's display of anger be ingredients for change? One day on the Big Island a Marine band, on its way to give a concert at Laupahoehoe School, drove past our classroom window. For some of the children it was the first time they'd seen a black person. They began to point, saying, "A black man, a black man," interspersed with negative comments.

So there I was once again, speaking to six-year-olds about unacceptable behavior. Perhaps it was only my anger and the passion in my voice that told them their behavior wasn't right. When they returned to the classroom after the concert, two of the boys announced, "Teacher, we waved to the Marines. Only the black one waved back. He was the nice one." They were trying and they were getting it, as was their teacher.

The following are excerpts from a letter I wrote to a five-year-old boy, grown up by then, and included in my book, *Teacher, You Look Like a Horse!*

Dear Alan,

You were in kindergarten when we first met. I walked out of that airplane on a hot blistering August Michigan day. I saw you, a serious little five-year-old boy, waiting for me with a bunch of assorted gladiolus in your arms. I recognized you from a snapshot your mother had sent. You came to me and said, "Aloha, Frances."

Your mother and I were also meeting for the first time. We were pen pals since the seventh grade, so we practically grew up together although miles apart. I lived with you and your family during my year of teaching in Jackson, distinguished by being the only Japanese person in the community and, for many, the first Japanese they ever saw. Reactions were widespread from the minister who blocked my path to offer me citizenship to your dad's mother who did not welcome me in her home.

I met you again, so to speak, when I had finished my year of teaching and was returning to Hawai'i. You said to me, "You don't look different anymore." "Oh," I asked, "how do I look?" "Well," you said, "you look like Frances!"

I have thought of that night, and often wonder, can all of our prejudices and fears of the unknown turn us to our humanity with something so simple as getting to know each other? Should we keep our first impressions of others whose customs, appearances and language appear strange until we are able to say, "You look like you." Thank you, Alan.

Love,
Frances

So no, being a woman is a total pleasure. Being a Japanese woman whose "different" is often perceived as inferior or threatening is a challenge I've tried to meet with dignity.

THE PORCH

I saw the flowers before I entered her room: a gigantic bouquet bursting with spring blossoms. The card attached to the bouquet bore my mother's name, nothing else. Next to the flowers was a gift bag filled with snacks made in Japan. A note on the gift bag read simply, "To Pride."

Pride. Why does that name ring a familiar bell? *Pride.* I should know what it means, but I can't quite make the connection. I sat with my mother, inhaling the fragrance of the flowers, then later wheeled her to the solarium for her lunch.

Pride. Who's Pride? I spoon fed my mother, then wheeled her back to her room. *Who's Pride?*

"Look at these beautiful flowers," I continued like a broken record. "Somebody brought you these flowers." Does Alzheimer's allow fragrance to penetrate the senses? I spent the afternoon reading while she napped. *Pride?*

In the middle of the night, the fog cleared. *Of course—Pride!* Only one person would know about my teenage affair with Pride on that uncensored porch.

The porch, two steps from the ground, was where I read books censored by my teachers. It was also the gathering place for neighborhood kids and adults to congregate after dinner and talk story. My father and his friends recounted the day's events or one of their fishing stories, slightly exaggerated, while we kids sat and listened or told our own stories. It was a time for feeling safe. There were no television screens or newspapers to link us to the outside world, except for the *Hilo Tribune-Herald* with yesterday's news. If there were enough of us kids, we played Steal Steal Stone, kanapio and other homemade games. The setting sun was our cue that the day was over. We slowly stopped our games and storytelling and stood to call it a day. "See you tomorrow!" followed each of the neighbor kids home, as we gathered the empty beer cans and saké cups, swept the empty shells of boiled peanuts off the porch and went indoors to light our kerosene lamps.

It was on this porch that I wrote my first story, dressed as Grace Metalious as she appears on the back cover of her best-selling book *Peyton Place*. "This is how writers write," I concluded. Like her, I wore a sweatshirt, lit a Winston cigarette, tapped ashes into a tuna can and began tapping on my portable typewriter. I would have added a glass of wine to perfect the worldly writer's image, if only we had wine instead of saké and beer. Like Grace Metalious, I made a lot of smoke that day.

My first story is forgotten, but it was on that porch that I found my own private haven of blue solitude after the school faculty imposed censorship on me when I was fourteen.

"I'm not a sex maniac!" I shouted to Miss Sato, anger concealing my shame.

"No, no," she said. "We're just concerned about you and want to help. We noticed your interest in sex, so at yesterday's faculty meeting the principal asked me to speak to you."

"What? You talked about me at the teachers' meeting? What did I do? What is this all about? What do you mean, my interest in sex?"

"Well, we noticed you've been reading books that are really too advanced for you."

"Like what?"

"Your English teacher saw you with a book called *Office Wife*."

"I got that book from the bookmobile last week. If I'm not allowed to read certain books, they shouldn't be there. You can't stop me from reading any book on that bookmobile!"

"Well, from now on, a teacher will have to be with you when the bookmobile comes. You can't borrow books from the bookmobile without our permission. And if you have any question or interest in things sexual, come and see me. After PE class would be a good time."

I walked off, deeply ashamed that the teachers considered me interested in sex, and went straight to my social studies teacher, whom I liked and trusted.

"Did you all talk about me at the teachers' meeting yesterday?" I asked.

"Oh," she said, "did Miss Sato speak to you? Yes, one of the teachers was concerned when she saw you with that *Office Wife* book, so she brought it up for discussion. Everyone felt that you should be getting the correct information if you're so interested in sex, so the principal assigned Miss Sato to talk to you."

"I don't need any counseling. Did anyone read this book? Did Miss Sato? Or the principal?"

"No, I don't think so."

"Then how can you all judge me without reading the book?"

"Please understand, Frances, the teachers mean well and are here to help you."

"I'm not a sex maniac, you know!" I walked away.

I didn't need any sex education. My Uncle Jun had often told me, "You're going to grow up to be beautiful, so always remember that it's the girl and not the boy who takes her panties off."

Office Wife was the story of an office boss in love with his secretary. There were no explicit scenes or physical intimacy between the two; it was just a simple, uncomplicated story of a man paying attention to a woman in his office. In today's library or bookshop, it would be found in the young adult section.

And so it began. The Censor Shadow was assigned to tail me at each bookmobile visit. Before checking out any book, I needed the Shadow's nod of approval. I made it a point to reach for books on the top shelves to give them something to monitor. One day the Shadow on duty was my science teacher, and I picked up Victor Hugo's *Les Misérables*. When he checked my book and said, "Oh, less miserable," I rolled my eyes and looked at him with all the sarcasm I could muster. "It's pronounced *Les Misérables*," I said. "It's French!"

But the Shadow couldn't stop me from reading. There are black-and-white photos of me holding books with their covers facing the camera: Ray Bradbury's *Fahrenheit 451*, *The Valley of Decision* by Marcia Davenport and *Pride's Castle* by Frank Yerby. But I was also wise enough to know that *Lady Chatterley's Lover*, *Tropic of Cancer* and *Fanny Hill* had to be read off-campus.

"Yeah," I told myself, "those guys would call a special emergency faculty meeting if they saw my secret book stash." I found these books on the bookshelf at home, so clearly the Shadow had no jurisdiction in our house.

Years later, the Shadow would reappear in the schools where I taught. In one of them, my third graders weren't allowed to read or borrow books beyond the shelf labeled Third Grade Level.

Earlier in my career in education, I helped develop the K–12 literature curriculum for the state of Hawai'i, so I was well equipped to take care of the Shadow and keep him closeted during my years in the classroom. "Only in school do we assign reading levels by age," was my ongoing lament.

Back in Kapoho, I hadn't needed to look far to find a place to read X-rated books. Right under my parents' eyes, I sat on the front porch and read whatever literature I could get my hands on. One of these books would later resolve the mystery of an anonymous bouquet of flowers. To my family, seeing me with books on the porch could only mean I was studying and learning. I heard pride in their voices when I was found reading.

"Where's Hideko?"

"Reading on the porch."

"She's studying. Leave her alone."

"That Hideko is always reading," the neighbors often commented to my parents. "How lucky that your children like to learn."

It was best that no one saw the earmarked pages in these books. When I lost my privacy on the porch, there was always the outhouse. By the time I was sixteen, reading *Office Wife* was like reading nursery rhymes.

The morning after the arrival of the mysterious bouquet of flowers in my mother's room, I made a few phone calls and finally heard a familiar voice at the other end of the line.

"Tom," I said. "You rascal, you. It took me all night to figure out 'Pride.' Thank you so much for the flowers and the snacks. I'd forgotten all about Pride."

He laughed. "How could you forget Pride? You were always reading on your porch, and I was there when you said you wanted to be called Pride. I think it was after a character in a book. I was the only one who took you seriously."

Pride's Castle by Frank Yerby—how could I forget that book? I was enamored of the protagonist Pride, who I felt epitomized the promise of life beyond Kapoho. Pride was a rogue, a robber baron with brazen contempt for human decency or moral restraint. He damned everything held honorable in the public eye. He was a despicable man, according to the book jacket. And best of all, he had a great passion for one woman. I reread *Pride's Castle* until the pages were discolored from handling. I became Pride. "Call me Pride," I said, and Tom did, until he left for the Marines.

We lived near the train station in Kapoho. Tom was the only kid in the village who owned a bicycle. Every summer and on weekends, he rode his bike across the village to our home. He was like family, except he never ate anything in our house. His refusal to join us at mealtimes remained a mystery; he always got on his bike and was gone for a few hours. He became a fly on our wall and knew a lot about our family. He heard arguments between my parents but never said a word—just quietly got on his bike and left. The following morning, he was back, right on schedule.

Tom was a fast-talking kid, and words rolled off his tongue without punctuation. "He talks a mile a minute," we said, as he entertained us for hours, teasing and joking without pause.

"Tengala, Tengala," we affectionately called him—an empty tin can making a lot of noise. He filled our house with laughter and joy and broke the monotony of family life.

After he joined the Marines at age eighteen, a photo of Tom in uniform graced our living room, until the chaos of Madame Pele and her lava flows scattered and buried so many artifacts—and relationships. Tommy had been one of them, until now.

He delivered the second bouquet when I was there in my mother's room. "I owe your mother a lot," he explained. "I spent most of my childhood at your house and your mother always welcomed me. I will never forget her."

Damn Alzheimer's. If only she could see the young Tom all grown up into this gray-haired man, bringing her flowers more than fifty years after their last goodbye when he left for the Marines.

Up to the day of my mother's death, bouquets arrived on Mother's Day and Valentine's Day, still without his name. Cryptic notes accompanied each bouquet: *To Mrs. K for being so kind to me in Kapoho. To Mrs. K for always welcoming the* waru bozu *[rascal] into her home.*

And with each bouquet, a little snack gift for Pride.

That house in Kapoho is gone now. During Kīlauea's destruction of Kapoho, the earthquakes split the property under our house. It took a year for the Red Cross to move our house to a new lot in Pāhoa. When we returned to live there, it seemed it had been slapped together without much thought. But the Red Cross workers had done what they could in a time of crisis and without being able to consult my parents. Still, whoever directed the relocation and reconstruction must have known how important that porch was, to me at least, because they rebuilt it nine steps off the ground—a porch with a panoramic view of ʻōhiʻa trees and our new neighbors' rooftops.

I was eighteen years old when Kīlauea first erupted. In Kapoho, Madame Pele's wrath permanently buried the Shadow, and the new porch offered me total freedom to choose any book that was available in the libraries and bookshops.

View From the Porch

On this porch she sat,
A two-year-old,
Shyly looking at the world,
A world filled with confusion.
A red train station, trains
Transporting sugarcane and passengers,
The constant flow of strangers,
Train engineers and conductors
Dropping by for a glass of water.
The constant move of people
Like ants on a picnic spread.
She sat and watched
And often escaped into the safety
Of her home when confusion
Overwhelmed her.

Years later, on this porch
She sat, her place of solitude
For romance novels and girlhood dreams.
The station, replaced by a post office,
Continued its buzz of people
Like bees darting in and out of a hive.
Clients of her mother, a dressmaker
Stepping up unto the porch.

On weekends, a visitors' information center
With tourists stopping for directions
To the famed Warm Springs.
When disrupted too often,
From her romantic escapes,
She retreated into the outhouse.

This porch, two steps from ground level,
Rose nine steps off the ground
When Madame Pele, with
A fiery eviction notice,
Forced the evacuation
Of family and house to a new locale.

Her constant returns as an adult,
To a new setting in another town,
Still found the porch her favorite place.
On a wooden rocking chair,
A mug of hot coffee in hand,
Her first Winston cigarette,
Greeted now by two large banyans,
Guarded by ʻōhiʻa trees,
Carpeted below by red ginger flowers.
A gardenia bush she planted years ago,
White ginger blossoms from roots she had dug
From roadsides, transplanted for her view from
    the porch.
Finches, sparrows, cardinals and noisy mynahs
Stealing silences.
It was still her porch.

Four years ago, her mother's stroke...
A wraparound ramp transforming the porch
Along with her mother...

Today she returned to the empty house
With her mother's ashes in an urn.
She sat on the porch on a plastic chaise lounge,
A mug of coffee from a neighbor's house.
The ramp now obstructs her view
To treetops, skies
And gridded scenes of what once was.

The porch, now just a porch,
The house, just a house.
Without her mother in residence,
It is no longer home.
No longer her porch.

I sit on a different porch in Sacramento now, watching youngsters walk by with electronic gadgets stuck to their faces or plugged into their ears. They don't see me but I see them, from behind my books.

THE EASTERN WAY

The old Buddhist priest offered me hot green tea before explaining why he'd invited me halfway across the Big Island to meet him. The room was sparsely furnished with a wooden table and two wooden chairs. I felt the chair beneath me as I tried to become a Japanese of his generation, sipping tea by holding the tiny teacup with both hands and bowing to suggest humility and gratitude. Between us lay my book of poems, *Sand Grains*.

I'd been living with both feet slightly off the ground since its publication—my first published book of poems! A six-year-old's dream, a final reality. *The Honolulu Advertiser* devoted a full page to its review. A bouquet of spring flowers from the mayor's office greeted me at the book signing. They called me poet. The blurb on the jacket cover read: *Here is a pervading sense of the essential aloneness of the human spirit, the core of being hidden behind a protective mask.* The poems were written as an alternative to driving into a tree after my first love, Robert, ended our relationship. Poem after poem examined the imperfection of men, the unfairness of life, my brokenness. I was young, searching for the woman I as to become. But why would any of that interest a Buddhist priest? Unless he wanted his book autographed?

Except for the sound of a nearby waterfall, the room was quiet. The old priest poured me a second cup of tea. I felt it settle in my stomach and spread through the rest of my body. He sat there carefully turning pages of my book, pausing now and then. I kept turning the teacup in my hands, waiting.

Finally, in halting English, he said, "Kakugawa-san, there is much pain in your life. Permit me to explain the difference between Western love and Eastern love. In Western love, when someone no longer loves you, you are taught to say, 'I must stop loving him since he doesn't love me back.' In Eastern love, we say, 'I will continue to love him whether he loves me or not.'"

After a long pause, he added, "Listen to the sound of the water, Kakugawa-san. Listen, and learn to flow with it. Learn to love and live the Eastern way."

I walked away with an indefinable joy. I wanted to weep for no reason at all. I wanted to embrace the entire world. Yes! I felt such freedom. Such power! I felt a huge burden of pain being lifted from my body. I felt strong and wise. Yes, I'll follow the Eastern way. I'll follow the flow of the river. I will let go of that romantic happily-ever-after notion found in novels and I will live life as it is. I will not be paralyzed any longer.

I rushed home to write a letter to Robert. I wished him a happy life, thanked him for all the deep emotions that I had discovered I was capable of feeling. I felt magnanimously wise, perhaps even wiser than him.

I was young. My heart would be broken many more times. "When I am dead," I said with arrogance, "write this on my tombstone: She lived fearlessly!"

Three more poetry books followed in as many years. My pen anchored me, kept me attached to the worst and best of times. I was a poet, fearless, I thought, and a far cry from the young woman who had written the poems the Buddhist priest had read.

My poetry reflected this slow and steady transformation. The process wasn't easy, as these lines reveal:

> …*my hungry heart beats,*
> *alone…like little gray wrens*
> *crying! to be fed…*
>
> …*she blooms, then clings*
> *till shriveled veins*
> *slowly burn*
> *her clutching hands…*
>
> …*forgive the truth I offered you*
> *when I said I love you.*
> *I love you…*
>
> *Do little fallen sparrows*
> *Damningly, painfully cry*
> *Of short-lived flights*
> *Over silver-foiled lakes*
> *And crayoned fields?*

Or do little fallen sparrows
Happily, gratefully whisper
I flew
As dusk slowly turns its head
And dry dead leaves
Lightly touch their statued backs?

For twenty-eight years I floated buoyantly on the ever-moving river of love the old priest had shown me. In spite of the pain and grief that accompanied love, there remained the poet, the essence of the person I perceived myself to be.

Then I hit a rock.

Fear, anxiety and feelings of helplessness swirled around me like a tornado. My mother had been diagnosed with Alzheimer's. I began to drown, loaded down with heavy gear, unable to swim this river that had become such a friend to me. I was barely treading water. How do I stop Alzheimer's? How do I stop this thief from invading my mother's life? How do I capture this vandal who was leaving undecipherable chalk marks on my mother's brain? I found myself in a dry riverbed.

One otherwise ordinary day—ordinary meaning my norm for bottomless pits—I was stuck in traffic, driving my mother back from her doctor's appointment, and answering her repeated question, "Where are we going?"

"Okasan," I groaned. "I don't know." She must have known it was time to be quiet, because soon the only sounds came from the radio and impatient drivers tooting their horns. We sat in silence, waiting for the traffic to move.

In our silence, the Buddhist priest appeared. Soon the sound of traffic was splashing on the rocks beneath a waterfall. The aroma of green tea filled the car. *Flow with the river. Flow with the river.* A horn honked, the light turned green. I took hold of the oar, exited at the next off-ramp and said, "Okasan, let's go get some tea and dessert."

From then on, whenever an obstruction appeared, I embraced it. Whatever Alzheimer's stole, we lived without. Whatever time was taken, a few minutes were retrieved to sip tea and watch steam from the cup dissipate into the air. With my mother at my side, I listened to the sound of water. We flowed to the end of our separate journeys with love, compassion and dignity, because in the East, water flows without obstruction.

WORDSWORTH AND ME

This is a long way from Kapoho. Look at all that traffic! No cane fields or dirt roads here. I can't believe I'm sitting here, waiting for someone who wants to publish my children's book. It's like being in the middle of a movie scene. Wow. That must be the publisher coming in the door.

He sat across from me at the College Inn near the University of Hawai'i. He looked at me for a long moment or two before saying, "You are very beautiful."

"Thank you," I murmured. I was surprised to see him take a copy of one of my old poetry books out of his briefcase.

"I read some of your poems and find them very Japanese and elegant. 'Sunday Afternoon' is one of my favorites. Will you read it to me?" He handed me a copy of *Golden Spike*.

I better play this right. Japanese and elegant. I can do this. Better not mess this up.

I took the book and began to read:

Sunday Afternoon

Silence grows louder,
Raindrops fall longer.
Clouds drop lower,
Winds sing gentler.
Rooms feel emptier,
The heart aches deeper.
The grass stands colder,
Steps walk slower.
It's Sunday
In the afternoon.

"That poem always gets to me," he pointed to his heart. "You captured Sunday afternoons just perfectly."

I can't believe this. He even likes my poems! Wordsworth, we are on a roll, you are going to be published! Maybe you'll even get the Caldecott Prize! Wouldn't that be something? We gotta think big, Wordsworth!

Wordsworth was the protagonist of my newest story. Wordsworth was a poet. And a mouse.

"I got one of the best illustrators for this book. He's done all my children's books. He's delighted with this story, too."

Hear that, Wordsworth? They like you. Yippee.

"Are you ready to order?" he asked gently, a publisher courting a writer. Me.

"Yes," I said. "Thank you."

I pretended not to hear him say under his breath, "She is so Japanese and subtle."

Pinch me, Wordsworth. Am I in a movie with a happy ending? This is the big time.

My four poetry books had been published by a company in Texas and in those days all correspondence was by snail mail. Now, here at the College Inn, talking in person with a book publisher was another step away from my Kapoho outhouse.

But then disaster struck. He called for the waitress.

"Hey, you! Come here. We're ready to order. Sheez, hope she understands English!"

The waitress came over, forcing a smile, and I tried to make eye contact with her, hoping somehow to let her know I wasn't really with him. Without looking at her, he demanded, "Get us some coffee first." Was this the same man who less than a minute ago had spoken to me with such respect and kindness? A man who had liked my poems?

"Oh, Frances," Wordsworth said. *"The only difference between this waitress and you are your jobs. How can you let someone like him publish our book?"*

But, Wordsworth, this is our big chance to be published. Remember how you got here? It's been five long years since I created you for that Hawai'i State Foundation on Culture and the Arts contest. You came in second place. Second place, Wordsworth! You know this is our big chance.

"How can you let a man who treats another person so rudely, who represents everything we are not, publish our book? Remember how you got here. Think back to 1941, when you and the enemy wore the same face. How did you feel then?"

I haven't forgotten, Wordsworth. When Americans addressed me as the enemy just because I looked Japanese, it changed my face forever. That "Hey, Jap" really hurt. I know all that, but now we need to focus on why we're here.

"Well, welcome to the Pearl Harbor Cafe, Frances."

I don't need a comedian right now.

"Remember, too, Frances, that Catholic priest who said you were going to hell for not being Catholic? Remember how you felt? Or even those years when you had to work as a live-in maid to support yourself in college?"

Gee, Wordsworth. Why bring that up now? I took care of that priest in college. Sure, I felt like a second-class citizen, sitting in the kitchen eating cold roast beef the day after their dinner parties. But this is publishing, Wordsworth.

"And there was the Uyeda Store. Remember? Tell me the story again, Frances."

The waitress walked away with our order. The publisher was looking through my manuscript, nodding.

All right. All right. I'm walking past Uyeda Store on my way home from school when I hear my name. There are four issei men and women sitting in front of the store. It's a good thing—or maybe not such a good thing—that I can understand their Japanese.

"The Kakugawa children are all smart, they'll be very successful."

"But the middle one, Hideko, that one won't amount to much."

"Yes, that one is different."

I don't need to hear the rest of the conversation. I hurry away, feeling ashamed. You just wait, I think. Someday all of you will be waiting in line to buy my books, because I'm going to be a writer!

"So, Frances, you do know how it feels to be shamed and disrespected."

Yes, I do, Wordsworth, but that one had a happy ending. When my third poetry book was published, the Pāhoa community honored me with an autograph party. People came with homemade dishes and asked me to read some of my poetry. Then they got into line to purchase my books. When I looked at the line, I saw the four issei from Uyeda Store. They didn't speak or read English, but there they were, each holding my book with both hands as though it was a thing to be honored. They bowed and offered it to me to be signed. They even said, "Kakugawa-san." When I thanked them, Wordsworth, I was thanking them for empowering my dream the day they insulted me.

"All right, Frances. How about D-U-M-B?"

You don't quit, do you? My fifth and sixth grade teacher's favorite words were, "Some people's children are so D-U-M-B." Each time I gave an incorrect answer or offered an off-the-wall opinion, I was crowned D-U-M-B. I didn't care, though, because I knew she, too, would someday be waiting in line to buy my books, most likely right behind the people from Uyeda Store!

"Frances," I heard the publisher say. "Do you want dessert? More coffee?"

"No, no, thank you."

"Everything looks good. I'll drop off your contract in a couple of days. We've got a winner here. We can get started on the illustrations as soon as you sign the contract." He left a dollar tip on the table and walked me out, his hand gently leading me toward the door.

We shook hands on the sidewalk and as I walked toward my car, I heard Wordsworth:

"*That waitress felt just like you in all your stories, Frances.*"

That waitress has to learn to get a thick skin, Wordsworth. I did. I worked hard to get out of Kapoho, and this book will take me even further away.

"*Maybe you're already too far away, Frances.*"

I put duct tape over Wordsworth's mouth and drove home. We stayed up most of the night on a seesaw, Wordsworth and I—up and down, up and down, high into the sky and down.

Do I return Wordsworth to my desk drawer again? But this is my big chance. That waitress must learn there will always be rude people around who will treat you like a non-person. The publisher's rudeness shouldn't cancel this chance to have my first children's book published. Maybe a prize-winning children's book.

Late the next morning I called the publisher.

"Frances! I was just about to call you. I have the contract all ready and want to drop it off at your apartment."

"Umm, I've decided not to publish the story right now."

"Frances, I thought we had a deal. Is it the advance check? We can talk about that."

"No, I'm sorry, I'm just not ready to do this. Would you send the manuscript back to me?"

"You're making a big mistake. Call me if you change your mind."

He was abruptly gone, speaking to the waitress once again, and I was no longer the beautiful Japanese poet. I returned Wordsworth to my desk drawer, and there he waited for more than thirty years.

Take a risk. Yes, take a risk.

In downtown Honolulu, I sit across the desk from my publisher—a different one after all these years—going over the final details of my new book, *Teacher, You Look Like a Horse!* Shaking, I take a deep breath and with legs and fingers crossed pull out the manuscript for *Wordsworth the Poet*.

Okay, Wordsworth, this is our chance.

"George, I want to read you a little story."

Without giving him time to reply, I begin to read. I glance up at him between paragraphs; he looks like a poker player who's been dealt a bad hand.

He doesn't like it. Oh shoot, Wordsworth, at least I tried.

I put the story down, unprepared to hear him say, "That's delightful, Frances! Yes, I'm definitely interested in publishing it, if that's what you're asking. In fact, I can see a whole series of books about this mouse who writes poetry."

Wordsworth and I dance our way home. "He's everything the other publisher wasn't," says the mouse. "A good listener and a gentleman too! Yes, yes, yes!"

And yes, *Wordsworth the Poet* is followed by three other books in the series, and each one earns a Best Children's Story award in the year of its publication.

GIRL OF KAPOHO

She breaks away,
Deaf to the voices
That call her name.
She drops the ball
At their feet
And walks toward the sea.

Ah, girl of Kapoho,
Who sits and watches
The ships at sea,
Are you on a ship
Sailing your dreams
Against the wind?
Ah, girl of Kapoho,
Don't you hear
The voice of your island
Beckoning you back
To her coral sand?

Return, return,
Lest you get tossed
From stern to bow
Into the sea.

Return, return,
From the lure of the sea
To my coral sand.

DEAR KAPOHO

When I was forty, the poet Georgia Heard asked me, "When did you start becoming a poet?"

"It began in Jackson, Michigan," I said, "where I lived in a cozy little attic like Emily Dickinson, above my pen pal and her family, teaching first graders in a nearby school. I looked out one afternoon and saw orange and red maple leaves slow dancing past my window. In the silence, I heard Roger Williams's 'Autumn Leaves,' the piano music and the scene outside the window merging into one. What a contrast to 'The Twist,' the dance music sweeping the country at the time. It was my first Michigan fall.

"When winter came, I looked out that same window and saw the ground covered in freshly fallen snow. I went outside, leaving my footprints behind me. As I walked and walked, I was greatly saddened, knowing I couldn't do anything about the beauty of my lone footprints in the mounds of snow. I didn't have the words, yet. I could only think of Longfellow's 'footprints on the sands of time.' But those words weren't mine. Did it begin then, that morning of my first winter when I ached helplessly for beauty?

"Or," I continued, "maybe it was that summer I fell in love. It was a time for poetry once again. I offered him, 'How Do I Love Thee?' by Elizabeth Barrett Browning and he handwrote 'The Road Not Taken' by Robert Frost. When we parted, I memorized poems from *Reflections on a Gift of Watermelon Pickle* and listened to Kui Lee's 'I'll Remember You.' To keep from dying, to keep from driving my car into one of the trees along the Pāhoa road, I began to write poems of things broken inside of me. The first volume of these poems was published in less than a year. It must have begun there, my genesis as a poet.

"Are you sure?" she asked. "How about your childhood?"

"Kapoho?" I asked. "Do you know what Kapoho was like? I did everything to get out of there."

"Perhaps," she said, "it's time to return."

So I'm back in Kapoho with a shovel, digging for memories and images. I will probably find only black lava rock and stinky outhouses…

I'm lying on my back on a branch on a tree at Pohoiki Beach near Kapoho. With every move I make to maintain my precarious balance, the rough kukui nut bark massages my back like a giant backscratcher. Book in hand, I watch the waves as they tumble onto the black sandy beach, mesmerized. I watch bodysurfers and swimmers sharing the pounding surf. I know what aloneness and silence mean even as the voices of the swimmers break into my tranquil space.

My reverie is interrupted by my mother's voice calling, "Time to eat!" and I scurry down to rice balls, fried Spam, fried hot dogs and potato-macaroni salad. I reach into the aluminum washtub filled with freezing water and chunks of ice and pull out a bottle of Coke.

After eating and resting, I go to the outhouse to change into my bathing suit. The stench makes me want to throw up. (Now, if it had been our own outhouse, it would have been different. Our family outhouse was my place of refuge, a sanctuary where I spent many hours reading whatever books or magazines I could get my hands on to avoid household chores.)

Now it's Monday morning and I'm walking to school barefoot, dressed in my oversized home-sewn dress, with my home-sewn schoolbag swung over one shoulder—the emperor's kidnapped daughter, mistakenly banished to this godforsaken village by a cruel twist of fate. Someday, I vow, I will walk into a dress shop, ignore the price tags and buy whatever I want. I'm dragging my feet as I approach my classroom, knowing I won't find much excitement or mystery there—especially in my teachers, who I knew by their first names long before they became my teachers. They are all young ladies from our village.

"Eh," I complain to anyone who will listen, "I bet kids in Hilo have fancy college-educated teachers, and here I'm stuck with teachers who only made it through high school. I wonder what city kids are learning. All they let us do here is read, or they read to us and then force us to grow vegetables to sell to the cafeteria." No one hears me.

Today is music day. Our entire music curriculum is contained in one volume: a vomit-colored book of Stephen Foster songs. (It's no wonder I would almost fail my basic music course in college years later. It was a good thing the professor was old and liked my poetry and I didn't have to sleep with him to pass the course.) For half an hour, we sing "Old Folks At Home," "Old Black Joe," "Massa's in De Cold Ground," "My Old Kentucky Home"—and also "Dixie" for good measure. These spirituals of sorrow and brokenness make me feel Kapoho isn't that bad. I could be standing on an auction block, for sale as a slave, or living in slave quarters with whiplash scars on my back.

I become a sucker for sad feelings and stories. A pulse begins to throb deep inside of me. I borrow books on slavery and human suffering, romance and relationships, to nourish this pulse. At home, we sing Japanese songs about soldiers calling out their mothers' names as they lay dying on battlefields. For the rest of my life, wars would nourish my own Stephen Foster soul.

This year I'm in the fifth–sixth grade combination class. Miss Fujii gives us a reading assignment to keep us busy for an hour or so while she teaches the sixth graders. I finish my work ahead of time and walk to her desk to hand in my assignment. I return to my desk. I stand and walk to the bookshelf to get a dictionary. I take the dictionary back to my desk and pretend to look for a word. I close the dictionary and walk to the shelf to return the book. I walk back to my desk, then get up to walk to the shelf for the dictionary again. I repeat this a few more times to entertain myself. My classmates bend their heads over their work.

Those heads jerk up at the sound of Miss Fujii's voice. "Frances!" she threatens, "If I see you walk one more time I'm going to glue you to your seat." I hear snickers from my classmates. I take my reading book and pencil and scribble a note on the first page. I pass the book to Kay, who sits on my right. Her shoulders shake as she reads my note: *I glue her to her own ass!*

Kay returns the book, still trying to contain her laughter. I'm on a roll. I rip a sheet from my notebook and scribble another note for my appreciative audience of one: *When she smile, she look like obake [a Japanese ghost woman]. Her teeth so ugly, I elect her the ugliest obake in the world. Her hair look like steel wool. No wonder she single.*

Kay snorts with laughter when she gets my note, scribbles a few words and gives it back to me. Miss Fujii's commanding voice stops me before I can read Kay's note.

"Frances! Bring those notes up to me right now!"

Nani, who sits behind me, is returning to her seat after going up to the teacher to whisper something in her ear. She passes me with a smirk on her face. I take both notes and the book up to Miss Fujii. I have no criminal smarts and obediently do as she asks; the thought of swallowing the evidence doesn't ever occur to me.

Miss Fujii reads them, then announces to the class, "Frances has been writing notes about her teacher instead of doing her work. Look, she even wrote in her reading book. How shall we punish her?"

The class immediately becomes a free-for-all of criminal court judges.

"Rubber hose!" a sixteen-year-old yells out. "Send her to the principal for the rubber hose!" Rumor has it that there is a rubber hose behind the principal's desk for use on the big bad kids—namely, the sixteen-year-olds who are retained in sixth grade until, by law, they're allowed to quit school. Nani is one of these students.

"Suspension!" another voice rings out. "Suspend her for a month!"

"Expel! Expel!"

"Yeah! Yeah!"

She sends me to the principal, Mrs. Iwasaki, who reads my notes, looks up at me and quietly says, "Frances, I want to teach you something today. If you had kept these notes in your head without writing them down on paper, there would be no proof of what you did. Next time, when you get upset with a teacher, just think your words. Don't write them down. I'm going to suspend you for one day. I need to do this because your teacher is very upset. Stay home tomorrow and when you return, apologize to her. I'm sure all will be fine after you apologize."

I return to my class, thinking of Miss Fujii and the "Some people's children are so D-U-M-B" with which she addresses me whenever I give incorrect answers. I'll bet Hilo teachers treat their students better than this—maybe like Mrs. Iwasaki, who seemed to be on my side.

"Frances is suspended!" spreads all over school.

Oh no, I panic, *I hope Paul keeps his mouth shut.* Lucky for me, my brother keeps my secret from my parents, and the next morning I awake with a stomachache and stay in bed all day. I pretend to swallow the black tar-like Japanese medication I'm given. I write a note of apology to Miss Fujii.

The next morning I put on my solemn and regretful Academy Award–worthy face and hand her the note. "I'll never do this again," I say.

She looks at me and asks simply, "Are you sure?"

It's a good thing she didn't ask what I had learned, or I would have told her, "No write, no get in trouble."

When I left the sixth grade, Miss Fujii's parting words to me were spoken in private: "Keep on writing. Don't ever stop writing."

Yeah, right. Why didn't she teach me how to become a poet from fancy textbooks?

I'll bet Elizabeth Barrett Browning never used an outhouse. Speaking of outhouses—hey, Elizabeth, here's one for you.

Outhouse

A house unpainted:
A corrugated roof, four walls.
A floor, six by two and a half.
A redwood seat with two round holes
Sized to fit two adult bottoms,

Balanced on used railroad ties,
Squared over a bottomless pit.
Here she sits and answers
Nature's call.

The fear of falling
Turns her knuckles white
As she holds on to the edge
Of the wooden seat.

It's a generic outhouse,
Unlike the neighbor's
Where their additional hole,
Though smaller,
Makes it a throne for three.

A wooden box against a wall,
Filled with square red wrappers,
Greets her with faint apple scent.
At arm's reach, torn sheets of
The Hilo Tribune-Herald
Hang on a nail.
On the floor, a backup supply,
Sears and Montgomery Ward,
Her Charmin.

Outside the door, a peach tree
Reaches toward the sky.
At blossom time,
The scent of peach petals
Loses to the stench.

No flies, no gnats, except for cockroaches
Dwell below, sometimes scurrying across her butt.

Dampness and heat create unspeakable odor
In a stranger's outhouse.
She gags and holds her breath
In other outhouses,
Races home when the need arises.
Home, Sweet Home.

Above all, it is her place of refuge,
A place where her need
For undisturbed solitude
Is unquestioned.

It is a place where she sits and reads
Books, comics, True Confessions
Cover to cover, along with gulps
Of Life in These United States.

When called to do the dishes
Or to start the rice.
She shouts from this redoubt,
"I stay in da toilet!"
It is a refusal she has perfected
After years of practice, respected
By neighbors and passersby.
What parent would dare
Call the empress
When nature's call came first?
It was the house of royalty.

So, Georgia Heard, maybe I started becoming a poet in the Kakugawa outhouse, where the joy of solitary reading overcame the powerful stench. I had so wanted Kapoho to be the Eden of my dreams, a place of perfection where my teachers were college graduates, my parents resembled the great heroes and heroines of literature, and classmates didn't tattle on me. I so wanted to learn how to write poetry from fancy textbooks like the ones they use in Hilo and New York City or even Paris. But it looks like I didn't need all those fancy books after all.

I put my shovel away for now.

THE NEW KAPOHO, 2018

Memoir writers are often accused of invading the privacy of others. "Did you write about me?" readers ask. "Is that woman my neighbor?" "Who were you writing about in that story?"

When my book *Kapoho: Memoir of a Modern Pompeii* was released in 2011, I feared I had invaded Kapoho's privacy. We all knew each other in the village; we didn't need names to recognize the players. There were only two families who had sent someone to the leper colony on Moloka'i, and I had written about them. There was only one family whose child had died after a tonsillectomy at age five, and I had written about that child's mother. There was only one family with a bicycle, and I had written about them.

I should have known that Kapoho would not be fickle or fearful about one of its own. No one accused me of shaming or exposing them. No one asked for the true identity of a character in the book. The doctor's daughter didn't ask me if the "Horse Doctor" was her father.

Appreciation is all I've heard from Kapohoans. On the local coconut wireless, I get comments like, "Can you believe someone from Kapoho became a writer? I cannot believe she wrote about us, she must be so smart. We are so lucky to have someone like her write about us. She saved Kapoho for us."

At my first book signing for *Kapoho*, three generations of the Nakamura family stood first in line. Their faces showed their pleasure at seeing their home and store on the cover of the book. They stood in silence, then whispered, "Thank you." The cover photo depicted part of Kapoho that was destroyed by lava in the late 1950s and early '60s. Whatever we had lacked in wealth and modern appliances, we made up for with neighborly love. What we may have lacked in education, Kapohoans more than made up for with wisdom. I felt this in their silence.

Years after the destruction of our old plantation village, a new Kapoho slowly evolved. Newcomers purchased old houses and lots, built modern homes and brought life back again.

Though the landscape no longer hosted the old familiar ways of my former home, Old Kapoho still whispered to those who stopped to listen. The newcomers used the book to learn of the history of the land they had settled.

One new resident promised to keep the human values that had been the heart of the old Kapoho. Another who lived along the shoreline said, "Your book changed my life. I leave the gate open so people can have access to the ocean. That ocean belongs to everyone. I promise we will live as the people of the old Kapoho did."

In 2018 it was time for folks to leave again. Pele rose from her long sleep to finish what she'd started sixty years earlier. Our old house lot is now buried under tons of lava, along with Green Lake and the rest of Kapoho and most of its shoreline. Pele is still actively pursuing a path of destruction. History is an ever-changing landscape, and if my village of Kapoho is anything, it is certainly its history.

There is, however, one feature of living in Kapoho that everyone, new or old, shares in common. No matter what your status or what kind of property you have, be it a mansion or a modest lot, the land you think you own really belongs to Pele. Everyone who lives in Kapoho knows that. People only get to live there as long as Pele wants them to. When the goddess says it's time to leave, that's it.

My last visit to Kapoho was a year before the 2018 flows. At that time mailboxes lined a newly paved road, showing that life was reasserting itself over the old blanket of lava. A woman in the old Nakamura house shared her ghost stories with me: "We live with a friendly ghost in our house." Where before there was only lava, now there were papaya farms, coconut trees heavy with fruit, and even traffic. There was a memorial of remembrance at the Kapoho cemetery, built by children whose family members were buried there. The old lighthouse was surrounded by lush green coconut fronds; its beacon still pointed toward the white-crested Pacific.

Years after I first left Kapoho with a nudge from Pele, I rejoiced and thanked her as many did. She gave me the shove I needed to pursue my dreams and escape with my pen in hand. In other parts of the country, other Kapohoans shared similar experiences. "Who would have thought I'd be living in California?" remarked one of the sisters from the old Okuda Store. Mrs. Nakamura was delighted: "For the first time I have electricity in our new place. Thank you, Pele." And there were always those who remained to welcome us back when we visited.

Today both Kapohos are gone—my old one and the newer settlement that took its place. What wasn't burned by the ongoing eruption will be perfectly preserved, but still gone forever. That, however, is not the end of the story. There will be a third Kapoho, and a fourth, and a fifth. How far in the future will this be? Who can say? But the fires of Pele will someday withdraw to their home deep inside Kīlauea, the lava-made soil will become rich and fertile again, and Pele's beacons of warmth and delight in the night sky will attract new visitors and residents, to wonder and settle under her watchful eyes.

Like the old Kapoho, from the rock of our culture and the resilience of our people, memories too are preserved deep beneath the hardened rock. They will flow as always in our stories and in books like this one. Someday they will break the surface of our former village and cover the landscape with new farms, fruited trees, cane and papaya, tropical forests and the dreams of a future for Kapoho children playing on sandy beaches. There will be stores and roads and indoor plumbing and electricity that finally arrived in our village—and none too soon. Electric vehicles and mobile phones and wonders unimaginable will be there too. Kapohoans, of course, will do what they have always done: fish in the ocean, wonder at the night sky and pay their respects to Pele, knowing all the while that what she so generously gives to the people of Kapoho, she will someday reclaim again as her own.

Thank you, Goddess Pele, for my Kapoho.

GLOSSARY

Bakatare stupid
Furo bath
Futon Japanese cotton-filled quilt
Haole Caucasian
Issei first-generation Japanese
Juzu Buddhist prayer beads
Kimotori supernatural monster in Japanese folklore
Mochi rice cake
Moxa mugwort herb
Nishime Japanese dish prepared with chicken and special vegetables
Obake Japanese ghost woman
ʻŌhiʻa native Hawaiian tree (*Metrosideros polymorpha*) producing lehua blossoms
Shoyu soy sauce
Steal Steal Stone in Kapoho, a children's game of tag using a rock
Sushi Japanese rice rolls
Ume pickled plum
Yaito burning moxa on specific places on the body as a cure for certain illnesses

ACKNOWLEDGMENTS

To Red Slider, who read my so-called final copies and said, "This is a good outline, now fill in the story!" To Linda Donahue, for smoothing out the rough edges. To Charles Pellegrino for his constant reminder: "Your new stories have to be as good as, or better than, 'Mrs. Honda's Beautiful Daughter,' in your first Kapoho book." To Mark Arax for asking, "Do you need that last sentence?" To Wayne Harada for keeping me alive as a writer in his column. To Watermark Publishing—George Engebretson for knowing what really works and Dawn Sakamoto and Duane Kurisu for their work behind the scenes. To readers who have asked, "What was life like after Kapoho?" And to all former, present and future residents of Kapoho. Thank you.

PUBLICATION NOTES

An expanded version of this book was previously published as *Echoes of Kapoho: A Memoir* (Watermark Publishing, 2019).

"The Unfinished Dance" was previously published in edited form in *Our Dance with Words* by Northern California Authors & Publishers (Pretty Road Press, 2015).

"Eh, You Tink You Haole?" was first published in *Bamboo Ridge, Issue 98* (2011) and was the California Writers Club's second-prize winner in 2009.

Born and raised in the village of Kapoho on the Big Island of Hawai'i, Frances H. Kakugawa is an internationally published author of sixteen books, who has received numerous awards from literary and family caregiving organizations—among them, the Hawai'i Book Publishers Association, Northern California Publishers & Authors, Mom's Choice Awards, Sunrise Ministry Foundation, California Writers Club and Hawai'i Pacific Gerontological Society. She has also been recognized by the Hawai'i Japanese Women's Society Foundation as one of the Outstanding Women of the 20th Century in Hawai'i. Frances has taught at schools in Michigan, Micronesia and Hawai'i, where she was a curriculum writer, teacher trainer and lecturer in the College of Education at the University of Hawai'i at Mānoa. She is a columnist for the *Hawai'i Herald*—the "Dear Frances" advice column for caregivers—and gives lectures, workshops and readings to schools and community groups nationwide on the subjects of caregiving, teaching, writing and poetry. She also facilitates a writing support group for caregivers in Sacramento, California, where she lives.

www.francesk.org

www.ingramcontent.com/pod-product-compliance
Lightning Source LLC
Chambersburg PA
CBHW062034120526
44592CB00036B/2087